PRAISE FOR *The Unspeakable Loss*

"This unique book explores the aftermath of the death of a child with wisdom, depth, and incredible love."

> —Kathlyn Hendricks, PhD, CEO, the Hendricks Institute, the Foundation for Conscious Living

"There can be few better guides to dealing with the death of a child. Nisha Zenoff has crafted a fresh and compelling book sharing practical advice and wisdom for those in early loss as well as those who are through the initial shock. It is an important read for friends, families, and therapists as well as the bereaved that are looking for support and seeking to transform their experience in positive ways."

> —Gloria C. Horsley, PhD, MFT, CNS, president and founder of Open to Hope Foundation

"This concise book will not only be invaluable to generations of mourners, but to the therapists and supporters who need guidance in how to be helpful in that most overwhelming of tragic times. I cannot recommend it too strongly."

> —John Edward Ruark, MD, Emeritus Fellow, American College of Psychiatrists, coauthor of *Dying Dignified*

"Every page of this thoughtful and open-hearted book soothes, reassures, and supports as it details the contours of healing from the unimaginable loss of a child. Nisha Zenoff's sure and steady voice reaches out in kindness to guide you."

> —Sylvia Boorstein, cofounder, Spirit Rock Meditation Center, author of *Happiness Is an Inside Job*

"It is a powerful read, addressing everything from the fact that we all mourn such tragedies differently, that our lives are significantly changed in many individual ways, [to] how to respect our own needs for mourning and what to NEVER SAY to someone who has suffered such a loss. This book is emotionally moving as well as intellectually informative."

> —Barbara Finn, PhD, CGP, FAGPA, adjunct clinical faculty, Stanford Department of Psychiatry

"*The Unspeakable Loss* reveals a deep wisdom that only comes from one who has gone through the fire. Nisha's words have an authenticity and authority that will resonate with broken-hearted parents around the world."

—Dennis Apple, MDiv, bereavement pastor, author of *Life After the Death of My Son*

"A common response from any parent whose child has died is that her life is over. Indeed, the life she once knew is over; however, a new life of greater meaning is reachable. Nisha's book gives bereaved parents this hope and understanding. Her book provides much needed support at this most difficult time."

—Carol Kearns, PhD, author of *Sugar Cookies and a Nightmare: How My Daughter's Death Taught Me the Meaning of Life*

"In Nisha's own powerful story and the experiences of others who have taken the same difficult journey, I became more aware of the remarkable resilience of human beings. Nisha's book is a gift that will touch anyone who has felt profound loss. Professionals who work in the healing fields will also benefit from the tools and insights she gives."

—Gay Hendricks, PhD, author of *The Big Leap* and coauthor, with Kathlyn Hendricks, PhD, of *Conscious Loving Ever After*

"Nisha Zenoff has done a remarkable job as an author, mother, and professional therapist of speaking the unspeakable, and of inspiring bereaved parents and families to believe that they can survive. This book will be a much appreciated addition to my grief resource library."

—Lee Pollak, LCSW, grief counselor and therapist

"The words from parents who experienced such loss are priceless, and Nisha's own hard-won wisdom soothes as it provides deep insight instead of platitudes. This book will help parents 'heal and deal' and find the strength to go on."

—Brenda Knight, author of *The Grateful Table* and *Be a Good in the World*

"*The Unspeakable Loss* is a compassionate and practical in-depth road map grieving people need to read after the death of a child. The compelling story of Nisha Zenoff's own loss, the words of other survivors, and her deep understanding of the grief process will guide the reader back to life, decidedly different, but a life that can be once again full of joy."

—Nancy Saltzman, PhD, speaker and award-winning author of *Radical Survivor*

the
unspeakable
loss

how do you live
after a child dies?

Support, Guidance, and Wisdom from Others
Who Have Been There

By Nisha Zenoff, PhD

Thank you to Sylvan Kamens and Rabbi Jack Riemer for permission to reprint the poem "We Remember Them."

Note: The information in this book is true and complete to the best of our knowledge. This book is intended only as an informative guide for those wishing to know more about health issues. In no way is this book intended to replace, countermand, or conflict with the advice given to you by your own physician. The ultimate decision concerning care should be made between you and your doctor. We strongly recommend you follow his or her advice. Information in this book is general and is offered with no guarantees on the part of the authors or Da Capo Lifelong Press. The authors and publisher disclaim all liability in connection with the use of this book.

Da Capo Lifelong Press
Hachette Book Group
1290 Avenue of the Americas
New York, NY 10104
www.dacapopress.com
@ DaCapoPress
Printed in the United States of America

First Edition: November 2017

Published by Da Capo Lifelong Press, an imprint of Perseus Books, LLC, a subsidiary of Hachette Book Group, Inc.

The publisher is not responsible for websites (or their content) that are not owned by the publisher.

Print book interior design by Amy Quinn

Library of Congress Cataloging-in-Publication Data

Names: Zenoff, Nisha, author.
Title: The unspeakable loss : how do you live after a child dies? / Nisha Zenoff.
Description: First Edition. | Boston : Da Capo Lifelong Books, 2017.
Identifiers: LCCN 2017029174| ISBN 9780738219752 (paperback) | ISBN 9780738219769 (ebook)
Subjects: LCSH: Children—Death. | Parental grief. | Loss (Psychology) | BISAC: SELF-HELP / Death, Grief, Bereavement. | FAMILY & RELATIONSHIPS / Death, Grief, Bereavement.
Classification: LCC BF575.G7 .Z46 2017 | DDC 155.9/3—dc23
LC record available at https://lccn.loc.gov/2017029174

LSC-C

10 9 8 7 6 5 4 3 2 1

Contents

Dedication   xi
Memorial   xiii
Preface   xvii

Introduction   1

Part 1:
Can I Survive?

My Story: The Doorbell Rings   11

What do I do with the feeling that I want
to die to be with my child?   14

How can I live for the rest of my life
with this much pain?   15

Will my tears ever stop?   17

Am I going crazy?   19

Will life ever feel worth living again?   21

How can I accept something so fundamentally,
horribly unfair?   23

How can I function when my brain is in a fog,
when I can't remember things or pay attention?   24

Will my body always feel so wracked with pain?   26

What if I can't "get over it" or "get on with life"
the way others think I should?   27

What can I do about these recurring flashbacks?   29

What if I can't stop thinking about my child,
or think I see him sometimes?   32

What if I find myself talking to my child?   34

How can anyone know how I feel?   36

How can I go on when I feel so estranged from
the world, from others, from myself, when
everything is so unreal?   38

What do I do with these feelings of bitterness?   39

How do I stop feeling so guilty?   42

How do I stop thinking "If only . . ."?   44

How do I cope with the terrible guilt and
remorse over my child's suicide?   46

What do I do with all my anger?   49

How can I maintain my faith in God
when I feel so angry?   51

What if faith is not an option?   53

Sometimes I imagine my child's presence.
What do I make of this?   55

PART 2:
WILL MY FAMILY SURVIVE?

My Story: Phone Calls   61

How can I be there for my other children when
I'm so preoccupied and in such pain?   65

What do my other children need from me now?   67

What are the special issues siblings face?   70

What if my child doesn't want to speak of
her brother or sister?   73

Will we ever get back to the way we were?   75

How can we cope with the changes in our family?   77

As a single parent, how can I cope with such a loss?   80

What do I do with this tremendous fear that
something will happen to my other child?   82

We lost our only child. How do we create a future?   84

Will I ever be able to see or hear about other people's
children without feeling jealous, angry, or resentful?   87

Will our marriage survive?   88

What if my partner and I are not in sync?   91

What are the special issues fathers face?   93

How can we feel sexual now?   96

How can we get through the holidays?   98

How do I share my feelings with others?   100

What do I do with these feelings of loneliness
or separation, the feeling that no one else
in the family understands?   102

How do I handle my parents' or other family
members' different ideas about grieving?   105

Part 3:
One Year and Beyond:
Where Am I Now?

My Story: Remembering Victor   109

How can I handle the first anniversary?   114

Who am I now?   116

Everyone expects me to be "better" after a year,
but what if I don't feel better?   118

Should I still be feeling this sad?   120

What if my marriage doesn't survive?   122

Where am I finding strength?   125

How can I continue to help my children cope?   128

How do we keep our child as a part of our family?   130

How can I protect my health as grief takes its toll?   133

What if I find myself working, eating, or drinking
too much?   135

What do I do when friends don't understand my
feelings or needs?   137

What if my relationship to my child
still feels unfinished?   139

How can I feel a psychic or spiritual connection
with my child?   141

How can my dreams help me?   144

How is my relationship to my God changing?   146

How do I find a new sense of meaning and
purpose in life?   148

PART 4:
AS THE YEARS GO BY,
WHAT CAN I EXPECT?

My Story: Windy Hill   153

When does the pain become bearable?   157

When is grieving finished?   160

What if I feel guilty about feeling better?   163

Will I begin to forget my child?   165

How can I keep my child with me over time?   167

What do I say when people ask how
many children I have?   171

How do I handle the continuing feelings of grief
and jealousy as I watch my friend's children grow?   173

What if depression and sadness still color my days?   175

What will strengthen my relationship with my
partner now?   178

What is it like to be a single bereaved parent
and thinking of a new relationship?   180

Who remembers my child?   183

How do I say good-bye to some old friends
and hello to new ones?   185

How have I changed?   187

Will I be reunited with my child?   190

How have my feelings about death changed?   192

What makes my life worth living?   194

Poem: "We Remember Them,"
by Sylvan Kamens and Rabbi Jack Riemer,
from *The Union Prayer Book*   199

*Appendix A: For Family and Friends: Wondering
What to Do or Say?*   201

*Should I call? How do I know what would
be most helpful?*   203

What do grieving people say helps the most?   205

*Should I continue to write notes or call even if
I don't hear back?*   206

What can I say that won't sound like a cliché?   206

*Are there certain words or phrases I should use or
not use when referring to my friend's child's death?*   207

Should I talk about my friend's child when I'm with her? 208

*Should I remember my friend's child's birthday
as I always did?*   209

*What if I'm finding my friend's emotions to
be too overwhelming?*   210

*What if I think my friend is not recovering as fast as
he should, or that he needs to think about other things?*   210

*Should I make suggestions for things that might help
my friend cope, such as a book to read or a grief group?*   211

*My friend is drinking more than usual
(eating too much, has stopped exercising, etc.),
but how can I bring that up at a time like this?*   211

What if I'm worried for my friend's well-being?   212

What if I'm feeling distant or unable to really connect? 212

How long will my friend grieve?   213

Appendix B: Suggested Reading   214
Appendix C: Resource List   217
Gratitudes   226

Although the world is full of suffering,
it is also full of the overcoming of it.

—Helen Keller

"There is nothing to fear; there is only love."

In memory of our beloved Victor
Victor Robinson Zenoff
July 1962–July 1980

This book is dedicated to bereaved parents and
families and to those who support them, with
love from my heart to yours, and to my family
and friends, whose love sustains me.

Memorial

In loving memory of our children, and all the children not named here, who will always be remembered and who teach us that love never dies.

Andrea Daniela "Dany" Aguirre
Dominic Clemente Aguis
Alana Teresa Alioto
John Christopher Alioto
Paula Frias Allende
Gabriella "Gabri" Aparicio
Dennis "Denny" Alan Apple
Kirk Arsenault
Daniel Ashkenazy
Michelle "Shelly" Barnes
Nathaniel "Nick" Eli Baylson
Lynnel Ravon Beck
Phillip Behuniak
Jenna Caprice Betti
Andrew "Andy" David Bonapart
Gabriel "Gabe" Louis Bouchard
Aaron Phillip Breiner
Emily Shenandoah Brightwood
Katharine Anne Caple
Zachary "Zach" Andrew Clayton
Gary Daitch
Bret Diamond
Baby girl Ehrenreich

Walter Irving Ehrenreich
Jacob "Jake" Freeman
Jeremy Michael Fulmer
Lori Gentry
Charles Harleigh Gordon
Jennifer Consigny Gordon
Jonathon "Jon" Gottlieb
Joshua Miles Hansen
Adam William Herzog
Seth Michael Herzog
Mark Christian Hornor
Mina Hornor
Christopher Robin Hotchkiss
Cynthia Mayer Idleman
Jordan McLeod Johnson
Lance John Juracka
Emma Kristen Kearns
Kristen "Krissie" Michele Kearns
Priya Khadalia
Kimberly Kilgroe
Shaun Kilgroe
Jacob "Jake" Klairmont
Dominic Careri Kulik
Michael James Levy
Lance Jay London
Joshua David Lord
Logan Robert Lunas
Richard "Dickie" Mannheimer, Jr.
Erik James Marks
Ari Benjamin Mazer
Kristina M. McCoy
Little Lady Lori Margo Meislin
Ashley Marie Pedersen
Daniel "Danny" Michael Picariello
Richard Lee Pollak
David "Dave" Pregerson
Kathryn "Kay" Raftenberg

Anthony Edward Reed
Carolyn Ann Reichling
Kendrick Reusch
Justin Daniel Reynolds
Jamie Rosengarden
Neva Raisel Rubenstein
Lara Rachel Rusky
Ashley White Samuels
Benjamin Patrick Scheuenstuhl
Daniel "Danny" Cahn Schwartz
Steven Joel Sotloff
Liz Shaw
Phillip Michael Silverman
Judith "Judy" Singer
Summer Skye
Morris "Moe" Slotin
Laure "Lori" Kleidman-Chodorow Smallwood
Lili Rachel Smith
Ryan Michael Soper
Daniel Justin Stark
Sean Patrick Sullivan
Andrea Johanna Taratoot
Raul Castells Valle
William Penn "Buffy" Whitehouse III
Roy James Wilson
Franklin Micah Wood
Michael Benjamin Zalkin

PREFACE

1950, Savannah, Georgia

I'm ten years old, a happy, skinny kid with a large, extended Jewish family, all living nearby. I'm visiting my Aunt Lena, my grandmother's sister. Her house is elegantly furnished, with sunlight streaming in. Aunt Lena covers my cheeks with kisses and pinches that sometimes hurt. Over her fireplace hangs an oversized color portrait of a handsome young man in a chestnut brown suit. His blue eyes stare down at me as I secretly steal glances at him.

When I ask my mother who that man is over the fireplace, she leans down and whispers, "*Shh*, I'll tell you when we leave. I don't want to talk about it now." On our way home, she explains in a hushed voice, "That young man was Aunt Lena's nineteen-year-old son Walter. He was killed in an automobile accident when returning to his army base during WWII. Aunt Lena never mentions his name or talks about him. We don't mention his name when we're visiting either because we don't want to make her more sad. We know she's sad because sometimes she goes into her bedroom, closes the door, and stays there for hours. We don't know what she does in there, and we don't ask."

Aunt Lena's daughter, Sara, later told me that after her older brother's death, her mother never again mentioned him by name. No one in their home did. Sara wasn't able to talk about the brother she loved and missed. When her own son was born many years later, she named him Walter in honor of her brother. Sadly, Aunt Lena could never bring herself to call her grandson by his name, calling him by a nickname, "Billy." I recently spoke with Walter, Aunt Lena's grandson, who is now sixty-three. He remembers the heavy silence that hung over Aunt Lena's house, and the oddness of being called "Billy." "[Walter] died and we could never talk about it. [My grandmother] was sort of numb. She never said a mean thing, but she was always very sad, never saw her laugh." The whole family felt the absence of Aunt Lena's son, expressed in a terrible silence and the unspoken reverberations of her grief. Walter's death in 1943 became the unspeakable loss in our family, creating a veil of secrecy, pain, and unresolved grief for three generations.

At the time my mother told me about Walter, the thought of Aunt Lena spending hours in her bedroom intrigued me. What did she do? Did she lie on her bed and weep? Did she hold pieces of his clothing or his favorite things? Did she talk to him? Did he come to her?

After my own seventeen-year-old son, Victor, died in a hiking accident in 1980, I came to understand her grief in a way I would never have chosen. I had an idea of what she might have been doing alone in her room. There were many times when, overwhelmed by pain, I needed to withdraw from others, well-meaning as they were. Alone, it was a relief not to worry about anyone else or their feelings. It was a time to be with my feelings, my inner spirituality, and to ask God, "How could you let this happen?" I could cry, sit, stare, write, pray, remember, and think undisturbed about Victor. I was also free to think about other things. My solitude was precious.

Yet solitude was only part of what I needed. I knew, early on, that our home was not going to be like Aunt Lena's. We were not going to erase Victor's name from our vocabulary. I couldn't help thinking of Aunt Lena in her loneliness and sorrow. My heart went out to her. I wanted to go back to that time when I was young, put my arms around her, and let her know I cared. I understood that speaking about someone who has died is a personal choice. For some, the simple mention of a name can be too painful to bear. But I knew that I didn't want to only sit in silent pain as Aunt Lena had.

A few months after Victor's death, I was impelled to call Sara to ask about her brother's death. "What did Aunt Lena do after Walter died?" I asked. "I want to do the opposite."

We both chuckled. But it was a crucial question, and Sara's answer was just as crucial. "Tell everyone to talk about their child," Sara said. "Tell them not to keep the silence, to bring the loved one into the conversation."

Before Victor died, I, like so many, hesitated to ask a close friend about the death of her daughter because I feared causing her pain. For years I had wanted to know about her experience yet was afraid to speak of it. Mitch Carmody, author and bereaved father of nine-year-old Kelly, his son who died of a brain tumor, said, "Our child dies a second time when no one speaks their name."

Now, in my own grief, I felt the importance of speaking. Our family talked about Victor, and eventually we laughed together at some of the funny stories we remembered. We included photos of him in our gallery of family photos. It felt right to integrate Victor's life and death into our home, to find the balance of having him with us and not.

However, years after Victor's death when my brother and sister-in-law lovingly named their son Victor in memory of my son, it took me months to feel comfortable referring to my new precious nephew by his name. I gained new empathy for Aunt Lena and how she tried to avoid pain by not saying or hearing Walter's name. To this day when we talk about Victor, there are times when I ask myself, *which one?*

Our relationships with our children do not end with their deaths. Our relationships change, they're transformed, but our children will always be with us. The Compassionate Friends, the largest and oldest nondenominational international bereavement organization in the United States, encourages bereaved parents, grandparents, and siblings to speak openly and frequently about their children who have died. When we speak the names of our loved ones, we keep them alive in memory and celebrate their lives. This book is about speaking, about remaining in connection with our loved ones as a way of healing our broken hearts.

Introduction

Recently, I spoke with Cindy, a mother whose six-year-old daughter Linda had died in a car accident just three weeks earlier. She asked me three questions:

> What do I do with the feeling that I want to die to be with my daughter?
> How can I live for the rest of my life with this much pain?
> Nisha, are you happy?

After I answered Cindy's first two questions, I told her the third question brought tears to my eyes. I can honestly say that, thirty-seven years after my son Victor's death, yes, I am happy. I am also sad sometimes, I grieve sometimes, and I miss Victor every day. But I have discovered that even with a broken heart, we can learn to laugh and embrace life again.

The death of a child is the worst trauma a parent can endure. When my son Victor died in a hiking accident in Yosemite in 1980, a week before his eighteenth birthday, I questioned how life could be worth living again. Overcome with a grief I'd never known, I doubted I would ever again feel joyous or loving or have peace of mind.

This entry from my journal shortly after Victor's death describes my feelings at the time: "The pain is too great; I can't take a full breath. There is a fire in my gut that feels like it will never stop burning. I beg for the fire in me to be snuffed out. My child is gone! I feel crazy. Will I ever return to my 'normal' self? Do I even want to? Life is not worth living without Victor! How do I bear the unbearable?"

Even though I was a therapist and grief counselor, psychological knowledge and clinical experience did little to soothe my devastation and pain. I made a vow at that time that if I lived through this loss—and at first, that seemed far from certain—I would learn as much as possible about how other bereaved parents find their way and share that knowledge with others. I wanted to talk to the real experts—parents who had been through what I was experiencing. How did they survive? I didn't think I could. What was their secret? Is survival really a miracle? The result of hard work? Simply the passage of time? Is it due to courage or luck? Does it require a leap of faith? It felt crucial that I solve the mystery of how parents could make their way through the bewildering land of parental loss.

My initial research involved interviewing thirty-two mothers, all of whom had experienced the sudden and unexpected death of a child, some less than a month before we spoke, others many years earlier. They generously shared their intimate feelings—their grief, confusion, struggles, and healing—in the hope of helping others. They told amazing stories, of miracles, unusual happenings, and those first glimmers of renewal and hope. And they asked questions, heart-wrenching, crucial questions:

"Who am I now without my child?" "How can I help my other children cope?" "Will my marriage survive?" "Will life ever feel worth living again?" "What is my purpose now?"

Over the years, as I counseled many grieving parents, similar questions arose over and over. Their questions were always urgent, driven by confusion and pain. Yet those questions were often wise beyond their knowledge. They reflect the core challenges of the grief process: how do we remake our relationship to ourselves, our partners and families, our communities, our faith or spirituality? Parents' questions go to the heart of what it is to grieve, to be reshaped by loss, and, ultimately, to reconfigure a life in positive, meaningful ways.

This book grew from the collective wisdom of the parents and family members I interviewed, my own experience, and that of the hundreds of mothers, fathers, and families I counseled over three decades of clinical practice as a grief counselor and psychotherapist. More recently, I interviewed another forty-six people, including parents whose children had died between five and fifty years earlier, siblings, grandparents, family members, and friends. (Some names have been changed to protect privacy.) The people I spoke with provided remarkable insight into the long-term course of grief and recovery, an area only beginning to be explored in the research literature. We now know that grief is not something one simply gets over. It is a life-altering, ever-evolving presence.

The shock of a child's death affects every aspect of being: physical, mental, psychological, and spiritual. Unfamiliar and erratic behavior, emotional outbursts, anger at the world and at those around you, problems remembering the simplest things, changes in relationships, a desire to die, questions about one's faith, and a host of other experiences are normal to the grieving process. Many parents experiencing loss are physically weakened and more susceptible to illness or other health issues. They may also suffer from post-traumatic stress disorder (PTSD). They must cope with feelings of guilt and responsibility, and adjust to a new family configuration. Marriages are challenged, as couples face the differing ways they cope with grief.

We each mourn differently. There is no one prescription for healing. You are going to find your own way. Some bereaved parents find it healing to be in the company of other bereaved parents. Others seek solitude. Some search for information or self-knowledge; others find activities that give them solace. Yet as I spoke with these remarkable parents, I realized that there is much that we share. There are patterns and commonalities in the experiences of bereaved parents. As we move through grief, there are touchstones along the way that many who have lost a child will recognize, as well as stories and questions that resonate with others who have experienced loss.

I did survive; I am surviving. Most of us do. And when we do, it seems as much a mystery as it does a miracle. Although it feels like time stops the moment your child dies and there's a terrible grief you fear is forever, trust me that you will be able to breathe freely one day, to appreciate the beauty surrounding you, and to live again. We have a great capacity to heal and transform our grief over time.

If you are in acute pain, this may seem impossible—even absurd—right now. The thirty-seven years since

Victor's death have given me the advantage of being able to look back and recognize changes I never thought would occur, changes I didn't think possible. As life goes on and the years pass, pain is altered and even disappears for large periods of time. It's surprising how and when that happens, but it does. It is possible to again feel joy and a renewed sense of purpose in life. It is even possible to thrive, though this may at first seem impossible to believe.

Part of the miracle for me was to realize and then acknowledge the positive effects Victor's death and my process of grieving had on my life. It's difficult to acknowledge that something good can result from traumatic loss. Yet, over the years, in addition to learning to live with Victor's death, I've come to realize that I have been transformed by this experience in unquestionably positive ways. I, like many of the bereaved parents I've encountered, have experienced unexpected changes in my beliefs about myself and what's important, about faith and the miracle of life. Grieving parents often report becoming more compassionate and focusing more clearly on what truly matters in life. Many bereaved parents make remarkable choices about how to live the rest of their lives. Researchers are only beginning to recognize and examine the potent way that grief can, uncannily, enrich and transform a life for the better. The transformative power of grief is a topic that deserves much more focus.

This book follows the progression of grief from the excruciating first days through our long-term healing, but the grief process is neither uniform nor linear. After some better days, we may find ourselves circling back to a place of indescribable pain. Another day, our dark mood lifts.

We circle forward and back in this dance of grief, with the only constant being change itself. I encourage you to respect your individual grief/healing process, to trust that you are healing as you are meant to.

Immediately after the death of a child, or any severe loss, it is unlikely that you will want to read at all. Your brain has undergone a severe trauma, and it takes time before you have the desire or ability to read. This book is structured to be used as needed. Feel free to skip around, read bite-sized pieces, or dive into those sections that feel most relevant to you. Pick it up when the time is right and when the words and experiences of others can be a balm.

I wrote this book for you. I want you to know that you are not alone, whether your child's death was last week or many decades ago. Others have walked this path and were able to embrace life again, and you can too. I also wrote this book for your family and friends who care for you and want to support you throughout your time of grief, even while dealing with their own shock and loss. These family and friends play a special role in times of bereavement and are an essential part of your daily story of grief. This book is also for the mental health professionals and caregivers who seek to understand and assist their patients, clients, and friends through times of loss.

During that first year when I was struggling to find the desire to live, Victor came to me in a dream and spoke: "Mom, don't be in a hurry to be here. When you are here, it's forever. We'll have all eternity together."

I began to understand this life as a brief moment in a longer, everlasting journey. My relationship with Victor did not end with his death. My love for him is alive in my heart. I am more in awe of life than ever before. Its preciousness increases.

Even though feeling gratitude for this gift of life might sound like an impossibility right now, may you discover for yourself, over time, that love makes the unbearable bearable, and that the words of wisdom spoken by others or yourself can be a part of that healing.

PART 1

CAN I SURVIVE?

MY STORY: THE DOORBELL RINGS

July 12, 1980, Atherton, California

    The doorbell rings.

    I'm home alone. It's 9:00 p.m. Saturday and I've just gone to bed, still feeling weak from inexplicably becoming sick earlier in the day while having lunch with my mother. It's probably someone coming for a preview of my garage sale advertised for tomorrow morning. I'm annoyed. Maybe they'll go away, I think. I'm watching *Saturday Night Live* as I promised my son Victor I would, and I don't want to get up.

    The doorbell rings more insistently. Why don't they go away?

    Suddenly a chill comes over me. I do a mental check of my family. My husband David is in Milwaukee at his high school reunion. My thirteen-year-old daughter Fay is at camp in the mountains. Andrew, fifteen, is in Israel traveling with a group of kids. Victor, seventeen, is hiking in Yosemite for a week. It's too early for any of them to be back. My heart beats faster as I push myself up, the doorbell ringing.

    I crack open the door and see a young policeman, a heavy belt of radios and equipment at his waist.

    "Are you Mrs. Zenoff?"

"Yes, what do you want?"

"Are you alone?"

"Why do you want to know if I'm alone?" It strikes me as a weird question.

The police officer shifts uncomfortably. "Because I have news for you, and I hope you're not alone."

"Who are you?" I'm feeling more and more frightened.

"The police. Do you have a son named Victor?"

I open the door and stare directly into his eyes. He looks much too kind to be bringing any bad news. I glance at his police ID, too nervous to look at it closely. He could be a fake, a thief. This could be a setup to rob my house.

I swallow. "Is my son okay?"

He lowers his eyes and shakes his head.

"What's wrong? Where is he? What's happened?"

The officer looks straight at me with a blank face. "There's been an accident."

"Where is he? Is he hurt?" Silence. The officer's compassionate eyes meet mine.

"Is he alive?" I whisper the words I'm too afraid to utter, my heart pounding wildly. In that moment I know Victor is dead. I know it. Deep inside, my body knows it. This stranger standing in the dark is telling me something I know—the absolute unthinkable truth that my child is dead.

"Oh my God, no! No!" I scream. But I know Victor is dead. "Where is he? What happened?"

The policeman, voice strained, tells me that Victor fell while hiking in Yosemite. He was running downhill on a narrow switchback. He tripped and fell 700 feet near Lower Yosemite Falls.

I know it is true. I stand paralyzed. Something cracks in my brain, my head, my heart, my gut, as if blown apart by a bomb. I'm not myself; I'm watching myself from a distance. I'm disintegrating, gone. He's grasping my arm.

Something snaps into focus. "Did it happen this afternoon around 3:00?"

"Yes." He narrows his eyes, puzzled. "How do you know?"

"I'm his mother. A mother knows," I state matter-of-factly.

That was the exact time when, out to lunch with my mother, I suddenly jumped up and ran to the street, nauseated and choking. I vomited and collapsed onto the curb. Too weak to get behind the wheel of the car, I asked my mother to drive me home. I had remained weak, feeling ill all evening.

A million questions flood my brain. "How do they know it's Victor? Who was with him? An accident? Suicide? Was he pushed? Who found him? Where is he now? I need to go to him. There must be some mistake. Where *is* he?"

• • •

What do I do with the feeling that I want to die to be with my child?

In the last month I have been trying not to go under. I have been so close to going under. He and I were like one. When he died, I died. I wanted to die to be with him.

—Hedda, age fifty, whose twenty-two-year-old son had died
from acute hepatitis while traveling two months earlier

Your feelings of wanting to die to be with your child are normal and natural after his or her death. Of course you want to be with your child. Many parents have expressed these same desires, and I felt this way myself. It is not uncommon to want to go to your child, to join your child in death so you can be together. When you feel that you also want to die, it is most likely because you want to be with your child and to feel no pain. These feelings represent your powerful resistance to being separated from your child. The words of Laura, a mother I spoke with after her fifteen-year-old daughter died from complications from Apert syndrome, a genetic disorder, are not unusual: "After Lili died, I just wanted to just melt into the ground myself and disappear. If I could have I would have just literally melted into the ground and found her and been buried next to her. That's how much I just wanted to be taken away with Lili. I did not want to have to survive without her."

Right now you are caught between two worlds. Yet somewhere within you, there is the smallest, tiniest place of hope, even though you may not know it is there. You have so much to live for here with those who love and need you. Eventually, with time, the feeling of wanting to die fades as life here becomes more tolerable and, yes, even pleasurable again.

Your feelings are not uncommon among bereaved parents. These feelings don't necessarily mean that you are suicidal or will become suicidal. It doesn't mean you want to leave the rest of your life. These scary, painful feelings will subside. Most grieving parents do wish at one time or another to be with their child who has died, but actual suicide among grieving parents is rare. No matter how deep their pain, they somehow sense that one day in the future life will again be worth living. If your suicidal feelings persist or frighten you, however, it is important to consult with a mental health professional or call a suicide prevention hotline. Free, confidential support is available 24/7 from the National Suicide Prevention Lifeline, 1-800-273-8255.

• • •

HOW CAN I LIVE FOR THE REST OF MY LIFE WITH THIS MUCH PAIN?

Sometimes I feel that great pain, the shock of his dying suddenly. I feel it in the whole chunk of my body. Even my bones are very soft and fragile and not together. Nothing is together. Or nothing is whole.

—Eileen, age fifty-six, whose thirty-one-year-old son had died in a plane crash four months earlier

You will not have to. This torturous physical and emotional pain you feel now will soften and ease with time.

Do you know what beach glass is? Think of how sharp glass is, and then how over the years the tides and the sand smooth and soften the edges—it's the same with your pain. The excruciating, unbearable pain that you are living in right now absolutely softens over the years, over time. Your body is filled now with that pain, and your whole identity is that you are a bereaved parent. Yet there is a wise intelligence or spirituality in each of us. This inner source is what enables us to experience love as well as grief. Ultimately, your body's innate wisdom will help you to heal.

This wisdom is accompanying you right now on your journey of healing. You are healing at this very moment, even in the midst of your deepest despair. You don't have to believe this now, or to feel it. But others who have walked this path promise this to you. We are here to light the way and give you a map for your journey. You are not alone.

When the pain is overwhelming, when your child's physical absence is more than you can bear, you can keep an image or vision of your child with you. You can hold her close in your memory forever. Find a quiet place where you can shut the door, close your eyes, and spend some time alone with your precious memory. Take yourself back to a special day that you and your child had together. Remember what you did that you both enjoyed, what your child said, how you felt. No one can take this away from you. You hold your child through your continued love, and you keep her with you through your memories. And keep in mind the beautiful words that one mother told me: "I know something that was really comforting to me that [a friend] said to me. She told me that I hold the memory of loving Franklin, but Franklin also holds the memory of being loved by me. I had never heard anyone say that. And there was something very comforting about knowing that my love for him, he continues to carry with him."

Anytime the missing is overwhelming, you can return to your time with your child. It helped me when I put one hand over my heart with the other hand resting gently on my belly, closed my eyes, and focused my love and thoughts on Victor. You might try this for yourself. Others have found it to be soothing and comforting. There is no limit to how often you can do this—as often as you want! The missing doesn't go away, but your pain changes over time. Your vital life force will return. Hold your child close and trust that your love for her will be the powerful force enabling you to one day feel that you are beginning to heal.

• • •

WILL MY TEARS EVER STOP?

My tears are important and necessary and will always be there. They come from my very soul. And they're really difficult to control. They come unbidden, and they're just real intense.

—Dinah, age forty-three, whose twenty-four-year-old son had died in a construction accident fourteen months earlier

It's only natural to feel like an emotional wreck after your child's death or to be in shock. Pamela AP's daughter Gabri very unexpectedly took her life at age seventeen, jumping off the Golden Gate Bridge in San Francisco. Pamela describes what she experienced: "The loss, the realization. You're in shock at first. And it's such a physical thing, you're just so aware of the way your emotions feel physically, and you're in shock. And then after that it's the realization that, you know, that's not going away." You may feel numb or as though you've lost control. Or that your emotions keep gushing out, even though you work hard to keep them in check. You may not want to talk with friends or even go to the grocery store because the smallest reminder brings a torrent of tears.

When I asked Pamela what helped her, she said, "You have to allow yourself to grieve and cry and be okay with that and give yourself the time to do it. That was my experience." Such important words. If you feel like crying, cry. If you feel like wailing, wail. If you need to change your routine or spend more time alone with your feelings, do so. One thing you might try is to give yourself the gift of solitude. Lie in a quiet, comfortable place where you won't be interrupted and let your breathing slow. Listen to the quiet or to the noises you hear around you: the slam of a car door, the footsteps in the next room, a plane's engine overhead. If this quiet moment brings a flood of tears, let them flow.

Notice the pain and tears moving through your body. Notice your belly, your heart, your throat, your face. Notice where in your body that knot of pain is the tightest. What causes your tears to increase or decrease? Simply being aware can be a way of taking care of yourself, and can often lead to a feeling of emotional release. Remind yourself that your tears are cleansing and nourishing and that every cell in your body needs nourishment right now.

With time and your attention, and the most challenging of all, your compassion for yourself, the pain that brings your tears can lessen. There will come a time when you can choose your moments of tears. You will be able to say to yourself, "I'll wait 'til later to cry." As incredible as that may sound to you now, it does happen eventually. And eventually you will have days when the tears do not well up at every moment.

You may have been taught that you must have full control over everything in your life, including your emotions. If so, then feeling out of control is an especially terrifying experience. The painful truth is, however, you have no more control over the existence of grief than you did over the death of your child. But you do have choice over what you do with it. You are in control of that!

• • •

Am I going crazy?

I don't like talking about it with anyone. It's the toughest thing! I start crying for no reason, I'm not myself, I can't think clearly. I feel nuts, like I'm losing my mind.

—Richard, age fifty-eight, whose nineteen-year-old son Eric had died of accidental overdose two months earlier

After a child dies, when you are devastated by pain and grief, you may feel in danger of losing your sanity. The ground has shifted, and the world as it used to be is gone. Expressions of grief may look or feel "crazy" to the person going through them and may be difficult for others to witness. The day after Victor died, I sat on the floor of his closet clutching his clothes against my body, rocking and sobbing for a long time. I needed to smell his clothes, to hold him close. I would have gone crazy if I *hadn't* done that. My husband, concerned about my sanity, called our friend Alan, a psychiatrist, who told him that my behavior was not crazy. Rather, it was a normal response to a terrible shock, and that he didn't need to calm me down. I should be left to grieve in my own way. It was not a time to be calm. *That* would have been crazy.

Severe grief is an extreme state, not an illness or a pathology. Grief disrupts all you thought you knew about yourself and life. The loss robs you of your touchstones and throws you into unknown territory. Be assured, you are not going crazy. In fact, if more people told the truth about their experience, others wouldn't think themselves crazy or weird. Feelings and actions that can be unsettling to others are a natural response to loss and are part of healing.

Maria had been unable to hold her eight-year-old son when he died in a car accident or to see his body. What she told me remains in my heart to this day: "One thing I did do, and I'm glad I did, was when the funeral home said they needed clothes for the body, I took the time to take his clothes that he was going to be wearing. And I chose clothes that he would feel comfortable in, plaid shirt and pair of jeans. I took and washed them by hand, hung them on the line. I sang. I sang to him while I was doing it. I took his clothes down. I took his shoes. I sat in the rocking chair and I rocked his clothes, just rocked his clothes and sang to him.

"They tried to get me to stop. They said, 'Oh, you're killing yourself. Look what you are doing to yourself.' I did just what I felt like doing, just exactly what I wanted to do. I just held the clothes and rocked him and sang, and sang, and sang. Sang lullabies. Hung them out on the line. It was a whole ritual. I took the time to do that, and thank God I did. Thank God I did. 'Cause that was my ritual. I put him to bed."

• • •

WILL LIFE EVER FEEL WORTH LIVING AGAIN?

Living seems like too much trouble. I just don't have the energy for it. Most of the time I feel so alone and so isolated. And yet there are a lot of people who care about me and who try.

—Madeline, age thirty-three, whose twelve-year-old daughter had died of leukemia four months earlier

The death of a child can be felt as a wound that cannot be healed. Someone with whom you shared the closest bond is gone. You face the agony of knowing you will never again see your child's face, hear her voice, hold her in your arms. You have lost not only your child, but that unique connection between you and your child. What you and your child had is irreplaceable.

Grieving parents are often angry, bitter, and depressed, fearing that their feelings of hopelessness and despair will last forever. They will not. However, since you do not yet truly know that, one of your biggest challenges is to learn to tolerate the depth of your own despair and to have compassion for your own suffering. In doing so, you give yourself permission to live your life one moment at a time, understanding that the pain you now feel will change.

This takes great courage, patience with yourself, and a leap of faith. It does not require that you know in advance that you will feel better. So give yourself permission to not know how you are going to get to there from here. You will find a way to bear the unbearable by going forward into the unknown. You do not have to know how to survive right now to succeed at doing so in the future. Just know that you can survive, and you will once again feel the comfort and beauty of being in the world.

Your work right now is to be compassionate with yourself and your pain. Be loving to yourself, as if you were taking care of your child, loving your child. Bring that love from your heart for yourself right now. If it helps, you can place both hands gently over your heart. Take three deep breaths and then breathe naturally and normally. Bring into your awareness an image of your loved one that brings you joy. Repeat, "I hold you in my heart with love forever." You can add, "I love you," or "Love is all there is." You can also improvise and add whatever words or phrases feel calming and nurturing. Repeat whatever words feel right to you, and offer them to yourself and to your child.

* * *

How can I accept something so fundamentally, horribly unfair?

I wanted to breathe life into her. I gave her life once, but I couldn't even try. I wasn't even given a chance. They took her from me and gave her back to me in a little box.

—Doris, age twenty-eight, whose two-month-old daughter had died of sudden infant death syndrome (SIDS) three months earlier

Because most parents assume their children will outlive them, a child's death brings a terrible shattering of the illusion we call "fairness." When a child dies, it is not fair, it is not right, and no amount of trying can make it feel right because, in fact, there is nothing right about it. When people who have not suffered the loss of a child talk of accepting your child's death, no one should assume this means feeling that the death of your child is acceptable. You never have to find it acceptable. You never, in all your healing work, have to accept that your child's death was right or fair. You will, as you move through your healing, come to a place where you understand that rightness and fairness are irrelevant to this journey of grief. I often consider these beautiful lines from Rainer Maria Rilke's book, *Letters to a Young Poet*: "Be patient toward all that is unsolved in your heart and try to love the questions themselves. Live the questions now. Perhaps you will gradually, without noticing it, live along some distant day into the answer."

• • •

How can I function when my brain is in a fog, when I can't remember things or pay attention?

I'm very confused in my thinking, very disorganized. I feel light-headed and fuzzy, out of control, and it frightens me.

—Dinah, age forty-three, whose twenty-four-year-old son had died in a construction accident fourteen months earlier

Grief can create confusion and disorientation, a feeling that your brain has been damaged by the shock. You may think, "I just can't concentrate," and find it nearly impossible to focus. You find yourself reading the same paragraph over and over, still not making sense of it. You may even think you are losing your mind or developing Alzheimer's. The simplest things you've always done automatically can be unfamiliar and perplexing. I remember driving my car one day after Victor's death. As I approached a red light, I became terribly confused. I could not remember what the red light *meant*. Should I stop or go? For a moment or two, I could not recall what to do.

Forgive yourself when you are not as reliable or responsible as you once were. Remember that you are suffering a deep wound, and that is where all your concentration and energy are going. Your body and mind are honed in on helping you survive the process of grief. This focus is exactly what your body and mind need, not whether you remembered to get carrots at the grocery store. When you think of your distraction in this way, you realize that your body is healing in exactly the way it needs to. Even though your forgetfulness and confusion can be worrying and embarrassing, your memory and concentration will return, no matter how unlikely that seems today.

If you want to help clear and calm your mind, meditation can be a powerful tool. I began meditating soon after Victor's death, and my meditation practice has been invaluable in helping me refocus and quiet the sometimes overwhelming noise, confusion, or negativity in my head. There are meditation groups and many excellent books that can help you develop a meditation practice, such as those by Jack Kornfield or Sylvia Boorstein in the Suggested Reading list, Appendix B. Right now, to begin, try this:

> Find a quiet place where you can sit or lie comfortably. Take several slow deep breaths, focusing on the full in-breath and then on the long exhale. Keep your attention focused on your slow breathing, feeling the breath at the tip of your nostrils going in and going out. Do this for as long as you feel able, whether thirty seconds or thirty minutes. Draw in a long inhale; slowly release the exhale, focusing only on your breath. If your mind wanders or intrusive thoughts interrupt, simply guide your focus back to your breath. Giving calm attention to your breathing in this way can help ease tension and stress in body and mind.

• • •

WILL MY BODY ALWAYS FEEL
SO WRACKED WITH PAIN?

It's like some big, scaly, ugly hand reaches down your throat
and grabs your guts and is just ripping them out.

—Betty, age forty, whose eighteen-year-old son had died in a
motorcycle accident sixteen months earlier

Many parents are surprised at the extent of their physical
pain during the first year after their child's death. They
feel not only tormented but also exhausted by the physical
pain sweeping their body. One mother said she felt as if
she had "broken bones all over." Another mother that I
spoke with described her experience like this: "I'm feeling
blown apart and shattered into pieces like a bursting hand
grenade inside my guts. My heart exploded. Broken into
pieces."

Even though your wounds may not be visible to
the human eye, they are there nevertheless. So be gentle and tender with yourself. Treat yourself with the care
a wounded person needs. Invisible wounds can be just as
real as visible ones. Grief can burn into the lining of your
stomach as painfully as the fires of grief burn into your
heart.

Headaches or heartaches, the pain you feel is your
body's invitation to pay attention to its messages. Instead
of worrying or trying to avoid these feelings, try to imagine that they are nature's way of gently asking, in the language of the body, for your attention. Do you need to slow
down and rest? To connect with your partner or reach out
to friends to share some of your feelings? To have a conversation with your God? Does your back hurt because

you've held yourself up for too long now and you need to lie down? Listen to what your body needs and give it attention.

As suggested in the previous pages, meditation and slow, deep breathing are a loving way to calm and clear your mind. These practices can soothe your body and release some of your pain as well: Sit or lie in a comfortable position in a quiet place where you won't be interrupted. Place one hand over your heart and the other over your abdomen at the navel. Pay attention to your breathing. If it's shallow, concentrate on taking easy breaths in and out. Take slow, deep breaths, filling your chest with each inhale, feeling the release with each slow exhale. You'll find these deep breaths cleansing and relaxing.

If your eyes feel especially tired or weak from stress and crying, close your eyes and place the fingers of both hands lightly across your eyelids. A warm compress across your eyes can also be soothing. If you feel like it, do your gentle, deep breathing while you're soothing your eyes.

• • •

WHAT IF I CAN'T "GET OVER IT" OR "GET ON WITH LIFE" THE WAY OTHERS THINK I SHOULD?

You're supposed to get over it in about six weeks and they all stop asking if you're okay. And they go back to work and you're supposed to go back to work and be normal and not cry anymore. People don't call and ask if you're all right or if you want to come to their house for dinner anymore. Everything is supposed to be okay and you're supposed

to get over it. The kid's dead, you know, and you can't
do anything about it or change it. I'd like to be one of
those old Italians where you put the black armband on
and say, "See this? It still hurts."

—Belinda, age forty, whose one-year-old daughter had
died after heart surgery nine months earlier

Tending to your emotional needs in the way that's right
for you is often one of the most difficult things to do, especially if those around you, who may not understand, are
suggesting that you do something different. You might
notice that there is a critical voice inside you or from others that says it's not okay to still be in such pain, to cry,
think constantly about your child, or feel unable to so-
cialize. If other people are expressing these same feelings,
it is easy to be intimidated by that inner voice that says
you should be recovering faster, or should stop thinking or
talking about your child so much, or should get out more.
When talking with bereaved parents, I heard so often the
feelings one mother expressed: "The scariest thing for me
is to be five years out, or even two years out, and have
people think it's supposed to be normal. It's not, it's just
not normal."

Psychologist Ronald Knapp, in his book, *Beyond En-
durance: When a Child Dies*, concludes that the death of
a child is the "ultimate human tragedy. . . . Barring the
death of a spouse after a long marriage, no other type of
loss even comes close to exacting the heavy out-pouring
of emotional anguish that child loss elicits." In fact, recent
research on parental grief has found that full return to the
life one had before a child's death, free of sadness, is not

a realistic or helpful goal. The "resilient, bounce-back" view can create unrealistic expectations in us and others. It can make bereaved parents think that they're somehow failing if they don't return within a brief time to their pre-trauma state.

A deeper understanding of grief allows us to see recovery as a lifelong process. Recovery involves learning to cope and to build a life of new meaning. It involves showing ourselves deep compassion, patience, understanding, and kindness. It is not something that can be rushed. Allowing your grief to take its own course will, with time, transform your present suffering into something more than sadness or pain.

You might try negotiating with that critical voice, within you or from others, that says you should be recovering faster, perhaps by picturing yourself talking to it. What does that critic actually say? How would you answer in your own words, defending your right to have any feelings that you have? Remember that although grief is difficult to live with, it is a completely natural process that exists to help you. Grief gives you an opening to work through your feelings and come to a place of healing.

• • •

WHAT CAN I DO ABOUT THESE RECURRING FLASHBACKS?

It was very hard for me to get past the images of seeing Nick in a coffin, and also seeing him after he died and then the

> funeral. It was very hard for me to get past the images from
> the funeral. And I felt it was very hard for me to focus on
> his life when I had so much trauma from his death.
>
> —Anna, age seventy-one, whose twenty-seven-year-old son
> had died of medical mismanagement twenty-three years ago

The memory of your child, as well as the vivid recollection of the death scene, is often lived over and over, like nonstop frozen frames of a movie. These traumatic, recurring images can make you feel stuck in a nightmare. They are a sign of your trauma, but they are not intractable. Fortunately, we now know a great deal about how trauma affects the brain and how to reduce these negative effects. There are many ways to treat trauma, but one method that has been well researched, especially since September 11, 2001, is eye movement desensitization and reprocessing (EMDR). It sounds like a mouthful, but basically it's a method of calming the autonomic nervous system, which is the primary mechanism for the fight-or-flight response. When your stomach clenches or your heart races in response to stress, these are signs that the autonomic nervous system is aroused. Other signs include being easily startled, feeling "on edge," or having angry outbursts or difficulty sleeping. EMDR can calm this arousal.

EMDR was extremely helpful to me. After Victor died, I kept having freeze-frame scenes come into my mind of his fall in Yosemite or his body in that horrible body bag. I couldn't stop these images from appearing until I started working with an EMDR practitioner.

Anna, a dear friend and colleague quoted above, also found EMDR to be what helped most in dealing with her traumatic flashbacks. "It was so profound because after working with [an EMDR teacher], every time I thought of my son I just thought of dancing with him. What had been in the foreground of my mind, the memories and trauma of my son's death, receded, and the positive memories of my son's life could come forth. My favorite, beautiful memories could now fill up the frontal lobe of my brain."

Anna described how EMDR works. "It's powerful because it still allows you to have your memories. It still allows you to feel grief. It allows your heart to stay open. But what it does is allows the death to be a piece of the person's life who died and a piece of your life, and not [take over]. It allows you to still connect to the [good] memories that you have of them. And that is so comforting for people."

Of course, EMDR is not for everyone, and many other practices can help as well, especially those that bypass the intellect or "mind." Because trauma is felt in the body, it can be released through the body, such as with massage, acupressure, deep breathing, yoga, dance/movement therapy, somatic experiencing, Rosen Method bodywork, and other forms of bodywork. Rhythmic exercise like walking, running, swimming, or dancing can help you focus on your body and what you're feeling in the moment rather than on difficult thoughts. Activities such as weight training, martial arts, rock climbing, skiing, or even boxing can also shift your focus. One parent told me, "I started crying in my boxing class the other day." The physical release of boxing brought emotional release, too.

Time itself is an important component of the healing process, and the sharpness and pain of recurring images will naturally lessen. Some parents might think, *Oh GREAT, EVERYONE says this.* They may have a hard time really believing it because their grief is so intrusive. I offer the example I mentioned before of a sharp piece of beach glass whose edges, over time, are rounded and softened. However, others may not want the pain of grief to subside because this decrease in discomfort might indicate an increasing distance between them and their child. Some might ask, "How can I hold on to my child, if not for the excruciating experience of grief?" But it is not time alone that heals. What we choose to do with our time makes a difference. If you want additional help, an experienced grief counselor will know how to work with trauma. And if you're interested in exploring EMDR, check the Suggested Reading in the back of this book.

• • •

WHAT IF I CAN'T STOP THINKING ABOUT MY CHILD, OR THINK I SEE HIM SOMETIMES?

> I can't stand it right now because it does overwhelm me. All I want to do is think about him. And it's such a painful process. The inability to put my emotions and my feelings that I had solely for him anywhere else. They don't transfer to my other children, to any of my other family, or my husband. They're just still there, that love, that physical need to put my arms around him.
>
> —Dinah, age forty-three, whose twenty-four-year-old son had died in a construction accident fourteen months earlier

It is completely understandable to think of your child often, even to become totally preoccupied with such thoughts. Many parents talk about how it is nearly impossible to get their children out of their minds. Ace, whose fifteen-year-old daughter Lili died six and a half years earlier, says, "There's not a day, not actually an hour, there are probably not minutes that go by when I don't think about her."

These preoccupations make perfect sense. Of course you yearn for some physical connection, some way to touch your child and feel her presence again in your life. Grieving parents often see their child everywhere. You may think you just saw your child in a crowd of children passing by. You may have been certain for a moment that you saw your child walk through a door. My son Andrew told me that for a couple of years after Victor died, "If I ever saw a bunch of long-haired kids who were around seventeen, I would think maybe Victor was going to be in that group, or like it was a bad joke or a surprise, that it couldn't be true."

Even though you rationally know that your child is not physically here in the world anymore, you are constantly on the lookout. You are hoping against hope that your child will somehow appear, however impossible that may seem. These moments reflect your habit of relating to your child, and, like all habits, this one is hard to break. Miriam said, "I miss him and I see him everywhere, you know. I see little kids he played with and stuff." These feelings are common to grieving. They are simply part of dealing with the shock and pain of your loss.

You may still have a powerful need to care for your child, to nurture him as you did before. One mother told this story, "I have a need to continue taking care of him. In fact, cutting the grass around his grave feels to me like I'm manicuring his nails just like I used to do when he was a little boy. After all, that's all I have left now." Nurturing acts like this one can be reassuring and healing. Caring gestures and rituals express your unbreakable bond with your child. Don't hesitate to embrace your child in your thoughts and dreams, to care for him and continue to hold him close.

• • •

WHAT IF I FIND MYSELF TALKING TO MY CHILD?

> I talk to him all day long. I'm constantly talking to him, constantly. My inner dialogue is all to him, and when I'm walking around the house I'm talking to him. I take him with me everywhere I go.
>
> —Susan G., age fifty-four, whose nineteen-year-old son Gabe had died of accidental overdose five months earlier

Cintia, whose eighteen-year-old daughter Dany was killed by gang violence, says this: "She loved to go to Taco Bell. I say, 'Come on, Dany, let's go to Taco Bell.' I talk to her all the time. I remember all the time. She hated vegetables. We laugh about things together. We cry together. If it is only left to me, I would stay in bed forever. I say, 'Let's go, Dany, you come with me today. Let's go, Honey, let's go.'"

Talking to your child is a way to keep your child in your life, a way to connect. Don't hesitate to speak to your child when the words appear in your mind or in your heart. This communication can be deeply healing. I was moved by the story that Lolly, whose eighteen-year-old daughter had died one year earlier in a car accident, told me: "And then I was walking along on the coast and I found some fantastic shells, just really great shells. All different shapes and colors and sizes. Clams and all kinds of wonderful things. And I felt really good. And when I was looking at these and seeing the beauty, discovering it where I didn't expect to see it, I'd go, 'Oh, Stacy,' because we both loved the ocean so much, 'did you put this there for me? Don't you love this one?' It was like there was real communication happening."

Communicating with your child affirms your continuing, vital bond. Or, as it did for Cintia, it can provide the motivation you need to get through your day. It can also provide a way for you to say some of those things you may have wanted to say before but somehow never did. Expressing love, pride, and even anger will help you to complete unfinished communication. This is especially important if you want understanding and forgiveness from your child. Feeling that you have said what is in your mind and heart moves you closer to being able one day to continue living your life in a positive way.

If you want to talk to your child, do it. Talk to him as often and as much as you want. Talk about your memories and stories. Tell him what you've been doing, what your family is doing. Tell him everything that's in your mind or heart. Ask him questions and listen to the answers. Or

write long letters or compose poetry—whatever it takes
for you to release what is in your heart and to continue
your bond.

· · ·

How can anyone know how I feel?

Lonely. Very, very lonely. And very sad. And I think that's
because of the pain. And I think that loneliness stems from
the fact that no one understands that kind of pain until
they've lost someone very dear to them.

—Lolly, age forty, whose eighteen-year-old daughter had
died in an automobile accident one year earlier

The last thing any bereaved parent wants to hear is, "I know
how you feel." Those who truly understand are those who,
like you, have experienced the death of a child. And even
they are only able to relate to your pain through their own
personal experience. There will always be unique facets to
your grief, some of which emerge from your unique relationship with your child, from who your child is to you,
and from what makes your child special. This specialness
can never be fully comprehended by others.

When your child dies, you've lost more than your child
in the present. You've also lost that connecting link experienced from the moment of your first bonding, whether
it was at conception, at birth or after that, or at adoption.
There are many layers to your grief, and you may feel
the impossibility of conveying to others what this death

means, how it feels. In some part, your grief will always be a private experience. Yet the hand of comfort offered by others is needed more than ever. While others may not fully understand, they may offer solace if you let them.

If you want to be with people who understand what you're going through as well as possible, this may be an excellent time to reach out to another grieving parent or to find a local grief support group. Please see the Resource List in Appendix C to find a support group in your area. These groups aren't for everyone. Some people feel too overwhelmed by their own grief to listen to the heartrending stories of others; some feel that they need to wait until their grief is less raw before attending a group. Some find that talking about their grief isn't what helps. But many parents gain a great deal of comfort and support from other bereaved parents. I know I did.

After Victor died, a bereaved mother invited me to go with her to a local meeting of The Compassionate Friends, a nondenominational self-help organization offering friendship, understanding, and hope to bereaved parents, adult siblings, and grandparents. There I felt understood. I met parents who were further along this path and who gave me hope and shared their healing stories. It was a meaningful experience for me, and still is. The friendships made through a bereavement group are like none other. It can be helpful initially to ask a good friend to go with you. And if you feel unable to reach out to a group now, perhaps you'll feel differently in the future. You'll know when or if the time is right.

● ● ●

How can I go on when I feel so estranged from the world, from others, from myself, when everything is so unreal?

I want people to know that I'm hurting. I walked into the butcher's a couple of weeks ago and I had been crying all day. I was buying some meat and he said, "Gee, you're stuffed up. Got a bad cold?" And I said, "No, my son died." It was like putting salve on a wound. You know, people's concern makes me feel better.

—Sharon, age fifty, whose twenty-one-year-old son had died in a boating accident nine months earlier

When you walk down the street, you may look like your usual self. Your hair is combed; you're dressed; your stride is recognizable. From the inside, however, in your heart and your gut, you know it's not really you anymore. The person everyone sees on the outside does not feel at all like you on the inside. Those people walking by cannot see the terrible wounds you now carry inside, nor can they begin to understand the torment suffusing your body. It is as if you are a burn victim who somehow has wounds that exist only beneath the skin. The trauma is invisible to others, yet you burn with pain. This disconnect between yourself and others can itself be a source of emotional pain, as you feel yourself isolated in another world, a parallel universe others cannot see. You feel at a distance from others, and ordinary connection can be difficult.

If you find you want to tell others about your loss and how you're feeling, by all means do so. If you'd rather be alone with your feelings, tell your family and friends that is what you need. Take the time to shut the bedroom door or go for a walk by yourself, to feel in communion with yourself and your child.

I've found that when I feel disconnected from myself or from others, doing something with my body or becoming more aware of my body helps. Getting a massage or taking a hot bath can be a source of comfort. Some type of calming exercise that you already enjoy, such as yoga or tai chi, can be a wonderful way to feel more rooted in your body. Breathing slowly and deeply or doing ten minutes of yoga stretches can restore a sense of connection to you. Or simply lie quietly, taking slow, gentle breaths. Sometimes I would lie on the ground to feel the solidity of the earth beneath me, the strong, supporting earth that nurtures us all. Remind yourself that you are a self in a body and that your body needs nurturing and attention as you grieve.

● ● ●

WHAT DO I DO WITH THESE FEELINGS OF BITTERNESS?

I know I've developed a real bitterness in me that I never thought would be there. It's not directed towards anyone, but I think it's directed towards life. How dare this happen!

—Lolly, age forty, whose eighteen-year-old daughter had died in an automobile accident one year earlier

Bitterness, like other forms of grief, must be fully felt, no matter how unpleasant that might be. When you try to ignore or bury feelings, especially the ones you don't like or are not proud of, they show up in other ways. Sometimes they emerge as physical problems or in relationship conflicts or in dreams. You may find you develop headaches or body pain, suffer from depression, overreact or even become violent, cry easily, eat too much, or lose your appetite. You can't simply make your feelings disappear. But you can learn from them and learn how to use them more productively. Anger, hostility, or bitterness use enormous amounts of energy when they are bottled up. Expressing them can take energy, too, and you may feel emotionally drained when you do. But the release of these emotions can help you to move forward in your grieving process.

Bonnie, whose eighteen-year-old son died in a car accident a few weeks before graduating from high school, remembered one of her aunts who had lost a son. "She was so bitter and angry, and really unless you were her immediate family she sort of didn't give a shit about you anymore. She was just so bitter, which made her have a very unhappy life. So I just felt like I had to make a decision, and I just decided within those first two years at some point if I was going to be stuck here without him, I was going to make a decision to not be bitter and miserable and to enjoy [life] as much as I can. And it's a decision. I think we make a decision."

The idea that you can decide not to be bitter may seem strange, even impossible right now. But be assured that the intense feelings you have now will ease. When I was overwhelmed with negative feelings, I remembered the words of Viktor Frankl, a Holocaust survivor who wrote so heartfully and articulately about how he and others rose above despair in a Nazi concentration camp. "We who lived in concentration camps can remember the men who walked through the huts comforting others, giving away their last piece of bread. They may have been few in number, but they offer sufficient proof that everything can be taken from a man but one thing: the last of the human freedoms—to choose one's attitude in any given set of circumstances, to choose one's own way." It is amazing that even in the midst of hell, when we feel that we have nothing left, there is still choice available. With Viktor Frankl as a guide, when my heart was filled with recrimination and pain, I would repeat the words: "I still have a choice. May I choose love. May I choose life."

The ultimate remedy for bitterness is forgiveness. Stephen Diamond, PhD, has written, "Bitterness is a chronic and pervasive state of smoldering resentment." When you find a place in your heart that can open to forgiveness—for your child, God, the medical profession, the driver of the car—those smoldering fires will die down. In the meantime, you owe it to yourself to have compassion for your feelings, even the ones that make you most uncomfortable. You can learn to accept bitterness as part of your grief without letting it control you or your actions. These feelings are a part of your healing process. Remind yourself, as often as you need to: *I can choose forgiveness. I can choose love.*

• • •

How do I stop feeling so guilty?

I told him to go to rehab or don't come home. The next thing I knew he was dead. How can I ever forgive myself?

—Randy, age fifty-three, whose twenty-two-year-old son had died in an automobile accident one month earlier

During the first year and well into the years that follow, the issue of guilt recurs again and again. Guilt can eat away at your spirit, making you miserable and sick. Feelings of guilt and blame can make you question how you can go on. One mother whose seventeen-year-old son died in an auto accident put it this way: "After the first month and the reality started to sink in, I thought, 'My God, what am I going to do with my life and how can I live?' And then I felt guilty that I was living and he had died. I think I was just in the pits, I was at the bottom. So I felt for a long time like I was being punished because I divorced my husband, or because I was mean, or somehow I must have done some cruel thing to people, something I was getting punished for from the universe."

Many parents are filled with self-recrimination, feeling that because they couldn't keep their child safe, they had somehow forsaken their duty as a parent. Monique, whose twenty-three-year-old daughter died by suicide, says, "When I get depressed, I think what a terrible mother I was. I start dwelling on all the stuff I failed to do. That's probably the major reason I get depressed." This tendency toward self-blame is unfortunately supported by our cultural context. In Western society—unlike in less developed countries where infant and child mortality is higher—the death of a child is unexpected. There simply is no context within which a child's death can be fitted. Without a larger context, it can be hard to understand or make sense of the death, which increases the likelihood that you will feel responsible or that you failed your child or failed as a parent.

If you wrestle with feelings of guilt or of being responsible for your child's death, know that you are not alone. Your struggles with these feelings are natural and understandable. Remind yourself that your feelings of guilt do not mean that you are responsible for your child's death. You are not. Rather, guilt and the pain it brings are an integral part of the grieving process. You may not get over these feelings, but like grief itself, they will ease, and you will come to a new relationship with them.

One way to release some of your feelings is to write them down. You might choose to make a list of things you feel guilty about. Don't worry about spelling or grammar. Don't edit your writing or set a time limit. Just write and write until you are ready to stop. Write as little or as much as you want. Do this for yourself. You don't need to share it with anyone else unless you choose to. Giving your thoughts written expression can help to discharge the energy behind them. Moving these thoughts from your mind to the page helps reduce their repetitive and all-consuming nature. You may find that writing from the heart in this way brings some surprises and releases some of your burden.

If you continue to feel overwhelmed by guilt, please find a qualified grief therapist in your community. This effort is worth it and can help to make this time more tolerable. If you don't have the energy to go online to find referrals or to make calls, ask a friend to do it. And remember to request that you be referred to someone who has considerable experience working with grief.

• • •

How do I stop thinking "If only . . ."?

I felt there was a lot more I could have done. A lot more.
I could have been with him instead of working all this
overtime and partying after work instead of coming home.

—Sonya, age forty-one, whose sixteen-year-old son had died
in a fall three years and two months earlier

The "If onlys" have probably arisen hundreds, if not thousands, of times since your child's death.

If only I hadn't put him on a bike so soon, he might
have learned to be more careful . . .
If only I had not let my child have the car, he would be
alive today . . .
If only I had taken her to the doctor sooner . . .
If only I had seen how depressed he was . . .
If only I had used a different doctor . . .
If only I was less strict . . . or more understanding . . .
or less impatient . . . or more supportive . . .
If only I left him alone about his choice of friends . . .
careers . . . hobbies . . .

Have you been looking for a cause, for some reason why it was your child who died? Have you asked hundreds of questions no one can answer? Almost every parent whose child has died has asked herself why it happened. The helplessness behind these questions, the feelings of loss of control, are especially searing. Feelings of regret and remorse, self-blame, and the intense desire to turn back the clock, to act based on what you now know, can be overwhelming. Hedda, whose son was traveling in Mexico and then decided to continue traveling in Asia rather than come home as planned, was overwhelmed with the thought that she had failed in her role as a mother. In Asia her son had taken sick with acute hepatitis and died. "So I just let him follow what he wanted to do. I don't know; everyone says I couldn't have stopped him. He was so determined to do this. And in a way, I was proud of him doing it. And every so often I'd think, 'Why did I let him go? Why didn't I insist he come home after his trip to Mexico?'"

There is no timetable or magic that tells your brain when to stop thinking these "if onlys." You will stop thinking these thoughts when they no longer serve your grieving and healing process. However, if you want to discharge some of the energy behind them, it can be helpful to acknowledge that you are thinking them—"I am thinking these thoughts again"—rather than pushing against or resisting them. That simple acknowledgment can defuse their force and repetitive nature. Instead of trying hard to stop your thoughts, I invite you to be willing to get to know your thoughts, to allow them expression in your head, or aloud, or in writing, drawing, or music.

I keep a basket of percussion instruments in my living room. Sometimes when my thoughts and feelings are overwhelming, I reach for my drums and bang away. The different instruments help me speak a language I wouldn't ordinarily speak. It's a great way to replace the incessant inner "What ifs" with a different rhythm. Of course, I make sure my husband and neighbors aren't around!

Keep asking all the questions you feel you have to ask, and know, at the same time, that you might never have the answers. Part of your pain is learning that you might have to live with the many unanswerable questions. You eventually learn to live your life with no answers, or maybe you find answers or even make up answers of your own that work for you. You may need to keep your heart and mind open to finding answers in ways you never imagined.

• • •

HOW DO I COPE WITH THE TERRIBLE GUILT AND REMORSE OVER MY CHILD'S SUICIDE?

Should've, could've, would've. Forget it.

—Simone, age forty-eight, whose twenty-one-year-old
son had died by suicide one year earlier

Kay Redfield Jamison, a writer and professor of psychiatry at the Johns Hopkins School of Medicine, who has struggled with bipolar illness and herself has attempted suicide, writes in her book *Night Falls Fast: Understanding Suicide*: "Suicide is a death like no other, and those who are left behind to struggle with it must confront a pain like no other. They are left with the shock and the unending 'what ifs.' They are left with anger and guilt and, now and again, a terrible sense of relief."

Sadly, Centers for Disease Control figures for 2014 show that suicide rates in the United States rose 24 percent from 1999 to 2014, with a 2014 total of 23,000 for all ages. Suicide is now a leading cause of death for those under age thirty-four. Though it's hard to pin down the reasons for this increase, drug use, economic downturns, and reluctance to ask for help are all suggested. Surviving parents often express the feeling that unless you have experienced a suicide of a child, you cannot possibly understand what they are going through: the guilt, shame, unanswered questions. Simone, the mother quoted above, says, "People don't understand the pain, the anguish, the illness. The illness is pervasive. It is not a one-off event. When people take their lives, except by accident, it is an illness. I've been surprised with some of the support we've received and I've been horrified by some of the lack of support that we have received."

Grief, of course, cannot be quantified or compared, and many types of death—whether they were homicides or were related to substance abuse, mental health, or HIV/AIDS—can, like suicide, carry a powerful stigma. Any stigmatized death is more likely to evoke a response from others that increases the stress and difficulties of the bereaved. If you are a suicide parent, you can be met with blame, of your child or yourself, instead of compassion, and social distancing and disapproval. You may feel judged, shamed, or humiliated or even be made to feel that your child's death is not worthy of mourning. You may feel haunted by the "what ifs" and feelings of failure. The anguish of one suicide parent I spoke with still haunts me: "I believe she would have lived," the mother said between tears. "I really believe she was just, with medication she would have lived. She just needed more serotonin for criminy sakes, is all. And I lost her forever because I didn't navigate that properly."

Remind yourself that your child's suicide does not define him, any more than it defines you. Hold close your memories of his life, his precious spirit and aspirations. And, when you feel able, I encourage you to find either a qualified grief counselor or a suicide support group or both. In support groups, parents who have been through a similar trauma can provide the understanding and guidance that is so crucial to healing. In addition to face-to-face groups, many parents turn to online support, such as www.parentsofsuicide.com, the largest online support group, and find it comforting to be able to access support whenever they need it. Empathetic, understanding communities of people who are committed to being there for you can be a lifeline, helping you to sort through your complex emotions and shift despair into a more positive focus.

In the meantime, even if there is only one thing that makes you feel calmer, more nurtured, more positive, I encourage you to do that one thing as much as you can. Whether it's reading, sitting in a garden, playing basketball, watching funny movies, or doing something to make someone else's life easier, when you find an activity that is positive for you, you're making a good choice.

. . .

WHAT DO I DO WITH ALL MY ANGER?

There was a lot of anger. I was mad at [my child]. I was
mad at the man who hit him. I still am because I think the
man should have moved over or slowed down. But that's
not going to change anything.

—Miriam, age thirty-three, whose six-year-old son had died
in an automobile accident one year and five months earlier

It is very likely that you feel angry about the death of your
child. You may feel angry at God, at yourself, at other
family members, at friends who don't "get it," at other
kids who may have had a role in your child's death, at the
child's doctor or teacher, at the grocery clerk, or at your
child himself. Anger can be as much a surprise to you as to
those around you, but it is a natural part of the grief process. A normally quiet, agreeable person might suddenly
have a very short fuse. Someone who is usually optimistic
and happy might become angry with the world.

Anger can be expressed in ways other than pure rage.
Someone sitting in one place without moving or speaking may be engulfed in anger. A person can be frozen by
anger into a terrible, punishing coldness. Women, especially, may cry when in reality they feel angry. Our society teaches us to fear our anger and irrational behavior,
and our culture can be especially unaccepting of wom-
en's anger. For men, anger is often seen as more acceptable
than tears, yet it is a cry of pain just as tears are.

When I talk with grieving parents, I tell them they're
entitled to all the anger they feel and more. And I encourage them to be aware of the hurt, loss, and pain behind

the anger. When you can identify what's behind your reactions, often the intense anger subsides. Ask yourself if
you're expecting too much of someone else or yourself, or
if your anger is a cover for other emotions, such as pow-
erlessness, disappointment, or fear. It's important not to
direct your anger at family members and, if you do, to
apologize. Remind yourself that they are hurting, too.
This is a time to be generous toward those around you
despite your pain.

Having a safe place to express your anger can help to
ease its grip. If you need to pound a pillow or tear up a
phone book, do so. Or find a place where you can express
that rage without holding back. Take a brisk walk or a
long run, go to the top of a mountain or to the ocean,
and yell as loudly as you want. I remember doing just that,
thinking the ocean or a mountain would be large enough
to hold my anger. I did feel relief but got a sore throat.

No matter how terrible this may seem, it is both natural and understandable to also feel anger toward your
child. Expressing it will not hurt your child and can help
to cleanse yourself of pain. Anger is part of your grieving
process, and acknowledging and expressing it can be a way
to lead you through your grief.

When you feel able, a powerful antidote to anger is to
turn anger into action, whether by helping other grieving parents or engaging in a cause that has meaning for
you. Susan G., whose nineteen-year-old-son Gabe struggled with the disease of addiction and died of an accidental
drug overdose, turned her grief into action by establishing
the Gabe Bouchard Foundation in honor of her son. The
foundation helps "Marin County youth who struggle with

the disease of addiction, their families and community, and shines a public spotlight on an increasingly deadly epidemic. The heart of the Gabe Bouchard Foundation is to provide compassionate, life-saving support and information to youth and their families." In this way Gabe's spirit lives on with positive purpose. When the time is right, you may think of a cause or purpose that tugs at your heart and motivates you to become involved. An engaged, purposeful heart will turn anger to good.

• • •

How can I maintain my faith in God when I feel so angry?

I'm angry with God. I feel I am committing a grievous sin
in being angry with God, who is supposed to be all good.
To do the worst thing you can do to people and just ask
them to accept and forgive it . . . it's a hideous thing to do.

—Dinah, age forty-three, whose twenty-four-year-old son
had died in a construction accident fourteen months earlier

In the face of your terrible loss, you may struggle to maintain the spiritual beliefs and practices that have always been a part of your life. Maintaining faith in a benevolent and personal God, one who watches over you and assists your well-being, can be especially difficult when you're aggrieved by the terrible injustice of your child's death. You may find the image of a loving God impossible to reconcile with what happened to your child. When I spoke with Belinda, whose one-year-old daughter had died after heart surgery, she expressed these difficult feelings: "Why, if there is a God, would he do something like this? If I'm such a bad and evil person, he should have done something to me and not to an innocent little kid like that."

If you find that your own feelings have changed in this way, I encourage you to remain open and trust that your sense of the spiritual will evolve. You may find another way to understand your life and what has happened, a new understanding that does make spiritual sense to you. Keep an open mind and an open heart. You may want to talk about your feelings with your rabbi/minister/priest/imam. He or she has heard this reaction before and can talk you through it, to help you reconcile and make peace with difficult feelings. I remember the wise words of Rabbi David Wolpe, of Sinai Temple in Los Angeles, who wrote a book titled *Making Loss Matter: Creating Meaning in Difficult Times.* He says that God is not about making bad things happen or making good things happen. "I know God is there when I have the strength to get through things that are difficult. There is no magic answer to loss. Nothing, not even time, will make the pain completely disappear. But loss is transformative. . . . [T]he blessing we seek in life is not to live without pain. It is to live so that our pain has meaning." This understanding struck me with great force, and I realized that when we accept these words, we are able to stay connected to our God despite our grief. Like all your work with grief and loss, the search for the spiritual and its deep meaning for you is also a process, and its mysteries remain an ongoing source of surprise and renewal.

• • •

WHAT IF FAITH IS NOT AN OPTION?

Atheism is a comfort to me. Not looking for god to explain
this to me. If I had become a bereaved momma with an
idea that "god's will" for my son had been severe mental
illness for most of his life and suicide, there would be
no end to my rage at that god. I am so, so glad I do
not have *that* to sort out.

—Nina, age fifty-two, whose twenty-two-year-old son
had died by suicide eight years earlier

For those who do not hold a particular faith, whose world-view is secular or materialist—up to 25 percent of adults in the United States—it is easy to feel uncomfortable when others talk of their faith sustaining them through crisis and grief. So much of the language of pain and healing is a language that invokes belief in a higher power. But of course there is no one way to heal, any more than there is one way to think about the world.

Though I'm someone who carries a strong faith in God, I have spoken with many people who do not share my faith, and I value their words. If you count yourself in this group, you know that you depend on the same things that parents who have faith depend on to heal your grief: loving and caring relationships, community, nature, pets, distraction, turning your grief into action to help others, deep breathing, a long run, a meal with friends. And most of all, LOVE. Love for your deceased child, love for your family, love of life. Love seems to be the constant in this grieving and healing process. Love heals our broken hearts, and there are many paths to follow to find this love, just as there are many ways to cope with and survive loss that don't involve religious faith.

I had a chance to speak with Peggi, whose son Jordan died by suicide at age nineteen in his dorm room after one year of college. She related how, seven years after her son's death, she attended a service for a great-nephew, Mark, one of six Marines killed in a helicopter crash while on a rescue mission to Nepal. When the military chaplain commended Mark's parents for their strength, attributing this strength to the Almighty, Peggi winced. She told me: "There is power in not believing in something supernatural. There is power in believing in yourself, your support system, and your ability to cope. When you think that this life is the only one we have and we need to make the best of it, you can infuse meaning in the things that happen to you. You can decide lessons you will learn from it. You can choose to make authenticity and kindness the essence of who you are. Personally, I can't think of a better way to live."

Peggi recommended a book by Greta Christina, called *Comforting Thoughts About Death That Have Nothing to Do with God*. In it, Greta writes: "I think that for all the comforting philosophies we can offer, the most powerful thing we can give each other in the face of death is companionship and witness." In all my conversations with bereaved parents, I have heard over and over this testament to the value of companionship and witness in a time of grief. I heard it from those who embraced a faith and those who did not. It is not a sentiment that depends on a religious perspective.

If faith is not where you look for comfort, I hope you do not feel alienated or alone because of your beliefs. The words of the parents in this book and the suggestions for healing are not tied to any particular religious or spiritual conviction. If you find yourself wanting a more secular conversation, there are many online resources—websites, chat rooms, even TED talks—where you can find like-minded people engaged in a secular conversation about grief.

• • •

SOMETIMES I IMAGINE MY CHILD'S PRESENCE. WHAT DO I MAKE OF THIS?

> I was on my back and I had my arm over my eyes. I was hurting and in pain, and crying hard. And all of a sudden it was black, but it was quiet. It was a different kind of quiet to me. And I just stopped crying and listened. And I was afraid to move my arm. I just didn't want to change anything. And I know I said out loud, "Bill?" because I really thought maybe he was there. That was the one time I really think he was there. I've tried to have that same feeling again and I've come close, which made me think that he is there. But it's not as dramatic as the first time you sense it.
>
> —Sharon, age fifty, whose twenty-one-year-old son had died in a boating accident nine months earlier

As part of the grief process, some parents have the powerful sensation that their child's spirit is near. Even parents who do not believe in an afterlife or do not think of themselves as particularly spiritual sometimes have profound experiences after their child's death of a presence, a communication, or an appearance by their child, in some form. It does not mean you are having delusions or that these experiences are the result of wishful thinking. Such after-death phenomena are found worldwide throughout all cultures and throughout the centuries. If you feel that connection, know that it is real even if it is not experienced by others in your family.

You may find that you often think of your child's soul or spirit, sometimes even believing you can see your child's spirit if you try. Some parents, often for the first time in their lives, pay attention to their dreams, go to psychics, or seek other ways to connect spiritually with their child. In the terrible weeks after Victor died, Victor's father, David, and I went to a couple of psychics. David recently told me that going to the psychics "opened the possibility there is another plane, which in turn caused me to wonder more about where Victor's soul is. I surely benefited from those two sessions with psychics and was comforted by them believing there could be another plane, and from what we were told having an image of Victor's soul and what he was then doing." Cheryl, who met with a psychic after the death of two of her children, said, "It didn't stop my grieving, obviously, but that pain and needing to take care of [them], not being able to, was really gone. And I really sense that difference in my grief from that point on."

Whatever label you use to refer to this connection, whether psychic or spiritual, feeling a strong bond with your child in this way can be profoundly important. Bertha, whose fifteen-year-old daughter died in an automobile accident, told me, "I do believe there's some spiritual phenomena going on. It's very warm and comforting, feeling her presence. If it makes me feel good, then it can't be wrong, and it's got to be right. It's got to be real."

If you have experienced this connection and the peace it brings, embrace and appreciate it for all that it provides. If you sense your child's presence, notice your feelings and sensations. Do you experience your child through your vision? Sounds? Smells? In your body? Through feelings that arise? Notice the details of your experience. Do you feel unnerved or comforted? Saddened or more hopeful? Perhaps you have all these feelings at once.

I sometimes experience Victor's presence by feeling his loving warmth, seeing his dimple and beautiful sparkling eyes. These feelings initially came unbidden and took me by surprise. Over time I've learned to call up his presence when I want to. This vision lives somewhere deep in my heart and helps me feel eternally connected to my son. It has not lessened over these many years but, in fact, has become clearer and stronger. What a gift and a blessing to know this beloved presence.

PART 2

WILL MY FAMILY SURVIVE?

MY STORY: PHONE CALLS

July 13, 1980, Atherton, California

The day feels like it has 100 hours. My chest is crushed
with pain, my breathing shallow. I can't take a deep breath.
The house is full of people talking and eating, and I am
wandering around, feeling lost and numb. My parents
have been with me since yesterday. I have been collapsed
on my bed, crying hysterically. Last night, I kept calling
the Yosemite ranger station, praying it was a mistake. I
kept asking the ranger, "How do you know it's Victor?"
After several hours, I went into Victor's room and crawled
into his waterbed. I could hear my parents sobbing in the
next room. When they arrived, I just looked at them and
said, "I can't take care of you now." I asked them to stay
in the other room. How could I be so heartless to them?
I don't want to know about their pain. I want to be alone
with mine. I want to be alone with Victor.

I called my cousin Margery in Atlanta. We grew up
close as sisters, maybe closer. We haven't seen each other
in years, and I want her near. I called my brother Elliott,
in Aspen. In my altered grief state, absurdly, I told him to
bring his running shoes and shorts as it's warm and sunny.
I called the Rabbi. He arrived quickly, young, his brown

eyes brimming with compassion. This is the first time he's
worked with a family whose child has died. Who can tell
us how to manage and what to do? All I want to do is cry
and scream. I want to go to Victor. He shouldn't be alone
in a morgue. That's no place for my son. I want to hold
him, make sure he isn't afraid. Make sure he's okay. I'm
dead and alive at the same time.

Mimi and Sheldon, longtime friends, arrive. We were
both pregnant at the same time. They lost their son shortly
after he was born. Maybe they can understand or help.

Finally my husband David arrives, to my great relief,
and we cling to each other, crying. He looks haggard, his
brow damp. The depth of sorrow in his eyes is searing.
The pressure in my chest is unbearable. I want to disappear, be snuffed out like a fire, the fire that never stops
burning in my gut.

How do we tell our other children, Fay and Andrew?
We have to bring them home. Where are they? I want
them here now. We go into the house to be practical and
make arrangements. We call the director at Skylake Ranch
Yosemite Camp and arrange to have them drive Fay halfway home and meet us in the parking lot of the Mariposa
Restaurant. I feel sick to my stomach.

"Don't tell Fay," we request. "We will tell her as soon
as we are together. Just tell her we want to visit with her."

A friend drives us. We're waiting in the drab parking
lot of the historic building, the oldest adobe in Mariposa.
I see Fay get out of a blue Buick, long-legged and tan in
white shorts, looking happy to see us, but bewildered. David is holding me up. We numbly stand in front of the
restaurant, our arms around Fay, sobs interrupting each
word I blurt out.

"Oh, Fay, there's been a terrible accident. It's Victor, it's Victor."

Fay stares at us uncomprehending while we tell her about Victor's accident and death. We do it the best way we know how. How do you tell your thirteen-year-old daughter that her best friend in the whole world, her oldest brother, has just been killed in a hiking accident? She sobs. We sit in the back seat with her and hold her all the way home. She tells us she had expected to see Victor, hoping the surprise visit would be with him. They adored each other. Three days later, Fay will receive a letter from Victor. A strange feeling. She will press it to her chest, teary. Victor and Fay were so close. He was her big brother, the oldest one. Fay was his baby sister. He looked after her and she looked up to him. He always took her side. She knew he loved her. There was no doubt.

We don't know how to tell Andrew, how not to shock or scare him. He's in Israel, halfway around the world. It will be such a trauma. Should he come home? Should he stay there? Should he decide for himself? Who would know what's best for a fifteen-year-old boy traveling with a bunch of kids? The unreality sweeps over me in waves. I beg for someone to tell me this isn't happening.

We call Israel and speak to the head of the youth tour group that Andrew is traveling with. Two hours later we call again and speak directly to Andrew. His voice, close to my ear, is familiar and comforting. Frightened, my heart pounding, not knowing how to say it, I blurt out, "Andrew, sweetheart, there has been an accident."

"Is Dad okay?" he asks.

"Dad is fine. But Victor is not. He's had an accident in Yosemite."

Silence.

"He's dead."

How could I have told him that way? There must have been a gentler way. Maybe there is never a better way to tell your son that his brother is dead. No mother should ever have to utter those words to her child. No brother should ever have to hear them. Andrew cries and says he wants to come home immediately.

"Mom, Mom, my nose is bleeding. I have a nose-bleed." His voice is startled, plaintive. Andrew never has nosebleeds. But Victor often did. "Mom, I can't believe *I* have a nosebleed." Is this a message from Victor? How mysterious!

"Before I come home I want to go to Jerusalem to the Western Wall of the Temple and write a prayer for Victor and place it in the wall."

I feel so touched and proud of him. He sounds brave and grown-up. I weep for him. My heart aches for his loss. I want to hold him and bring him home as quickly as possible.

We postpone the funeral till he arrives. What funeral? My head is spinning. There must be some mistake. Maybe Victor will walk in the front door. Maybe he'll call and say, "Hi, Mom." God, I want to hear his voice! None of this makes any sense.

• • •

How can I be there for my other children when I'm so preoccupied and in such pain?

I think that I looked at the girls and realized, "They're still here!" I was afraid maybe by that point I had driven them away or maybe [I had been] a lousy mother. I all of a sudden opened my eyes and realized, "There's other lives here. Just because one is gone, why devote my energy to nothing?" I mean, I'm devoting all my energies to being depressed.

—Miriam, age thirty-three, whose six-year-old son had died in an automobile accident one year and five months earlier

I'll never forget Anna's story of her twenty-seven-year-old son's death from medical mismanagement. She described her other son, six years younger, the gathering at the funeral home, her son's open casket. "One part of me was comforting one child and the other part of me was holding my other's child's head in my arms who had died. And I was thinking, I am [in] this parallel reality of being fully with this child who died. I had gone to another dimension with his death, and here I have to be completely present to my [other] child." I still think of Anna, one arm in the casket, cradling the dead, and one arm cradling the living. How do we continue to be a parent when we are caught between worlds?

As I think of my own surviving children, Fay and Andrew, I wonder, was there something that my husband and I missed as parents during those years after Victor's death? How could we be good parents when we were hurting so deeply? We had failed to achieve the very essence of parenting. We had failed to keep one of our children alive.

Did we actually stop parenting our other children? We certainly believed at the time we were doing all we could. We thought we were quite conscious and aware, even through all our grief. But I must admit that something in us definitely came to a halt. We spent a lot of time going through the motions.

If you have other children, your surviving children may be your reason to keep going. They still need you, and they provide ongoing meaning to your life, even if you feel emotionally drained and exhausted. Their faces greet you each day as a stark reminder of the extraordinary reality: life goes on. But for some parents, continuing to nurture their children is actually quite difficult. Pamela Ashkenazy, a bereaved parent and friend of mine who works with grieving parents, says: "It can actually be very difficult for them to be in relationship with the young child or an adult child because that child of course wants them to be in their mother role as opposed to, you know, shared grieving."

The pull between your need to mourn and your children's need to be taken care of is a tough issue, and one that shouldn't be taken lightly. Don't beat yourself up if you have had emotions similar to this mother I spoke with: "You know, I had other kids, and I just really didn't care about them at the time. He was my favorite. He was the one that always would come in. He'd know when I was feeling down. He'd just come in and make me happy. So I dwelt on how unfair it was. But now, the more I look at it. . . ." This is a time to be gentle and compassionate with yourself. You are bearing a huge burden, and carrying that heavy sack on your back has an impact. It's unrealistic to think it won't affect your parenting.

As a parent, care of your children begins with self-care. It's important to do what you can for yourself so that you'll be able to be there for others. Take some time to be alone when you need to, even if you can only grab ten minutes at the end of your workday to sit in a quiet place and do some deep breathing. Take a walk to pull fresh air into your lungs. This simple act can clear a foggy head, ease some of your aches, and make it easier to give your child a hug when you walk in the door. Then you can try to consciously set aside time to give your children extra attention. When each child feels that your attention is turned to him, whether to play a favorite board game, sit and talk before bedtime, or watch a favorite show together, he will feel calmer and more secure.

• • •

WHAT DO MY OTHER CHILDREN NEED FROM ME NOW?

I want [my other son] to have a good life and I don't want him to have a sick mother, an unhappy mother, a depressed mother. I wanted him to have what he always had, a cheerful, pleasant, enjoyable mother.

—Hedda, age fifty, whose twenty-two-year-old son had died from acute hepatitis while traveling two months earlier

If you have other children, they may run out to play with friends, laugh and go for bike rides, and continue with those wonderful activities, seeming as if nothing has happened. Children have the capacity to go on with their lives, to find active ways to burn off some of those emotions adults carry around. But something has changed, and they know it. Children grieve, too, and they do so profoundly. Unusual moodiness, withdrawal, problems at school, or anger, arguments, and conflict with parents and siblings can all be signs of your child's grief.

There *are* things you can do to help ease the pain of your child's sadness and loneliness. Sometimes a gentle touch and an understanding ear can be just what your child needs. You can help your children to recognize the various ways they express their feelings, perhaps through irritability and anger, or crying, or distance and silence. Is your child staying away from home more or listening to music in her room with the door closed much of the time? Simply noticing that your child is being more argumentative or challenging than usual, and commenting in a descriptive, nonjudgmental way, can reduce tension: "I notice that you've been getting angry a lot lately. I wonder if you're feeling sad inside." Helping your child to be aware of his own emotions is a simple gift. It lets him know that you're noticing what's going on for him; you're paying attention, which is a fundamental expression of caring and love.

Being honest and open with your children, in an age-appropriate way, about your own feelings can help. This lets your children know that being open about feelings is acceptable, and may make it easier for them to share what's going on inside. Pamela AP, whose daughter took her life at age seventeen, told me how she expressed her feelings to her nineteen-year-old son Nico.

Every once in a while in the beginning I would speak the truth about one single thing at a time, like if it had to do with her death and my feelings about it. I would say that I was having a really bad day or I was really sad today thinking of her because it was, you know, she should have been graduating this day or something. But I just left it at that. I didn't do anything more than just the statement so he knew that I wasn't super-woman, and yet I wouldn't go down into exactly what I felt and upset him that he didn't have his mother, that he lost his mother, too.

Kids don't want to feel overwhelmed by their parents' grieving. They want to know that their parents are stable and healthy, that they're going to live and to be there for them. They need to see that their parents are able to cope despite deep pain and that their family life will continue. Be patient with yourself if you're not always able to find the perfect balance as you walk that tightrope between your needs and feelings and your child's.

It's important not to direct negative or painful feelings toward others in the family in an unkind way, not to express them in ways that are destructive. As long as you and your children are making this effort, whatever you continue to feel and express is the right way to grieve for you. And if you feel that any of your family members need more help than you can give, find a grief group, spiritual counselor, or licensed professional who can help. This is a time to ask for support.

If your child who died was a twin, your other twin may experience particularly intense repercussions. Recently I spoke with a friend whose forty-five-year-old twin brother died suddenly on a golf course of a heart attack. She said, "Half my heart is gone." Twins have their own unique responses and issues in the face of such a loss. Please be aware that there are support groups that specialize in helping twins. See the website, www.twinlesstwins.org.

. . .

WHAT ARE THE SPECIAL ISSUES SIBLINGS FACE?

I think siblings are this silent population who don't get the focus.

—Susan L., age forty-nine, whose sixteen-year-old brother had died of medical mismanagement of a congenital condition thirty-six years earlier

I was fortunate to be able to speak with Susan L., who lost a brother when she was thirteen and is still, thirty-six years later, trying to understand how his death has affected her. She talked about the need for siblings to feel that they can ask their parents questions. "You know, can I ask you questions, can I talk to you about my feelings, about my brother who was lost? Will that hurt you? I think that's an important question for [siblings] to hear the answer to, and to give them a voice because I just assumed I couldn't talk about it."

I told Susan about a conversation I had recently with my daughter Fay, who said she remembers that my grief was the biggest grief, and therefore she didn't have a place to express her own grief. My close friend Judi recalls coming to our house right after she'd heard of Victor's death. "I remember the children," she said. "I remember Fay and Andrew being like ghosts walking around. They were so sad and in shock. And I think so much of the attention was going to you and David [Victor's father], and everyone who was there was in their own grief. I just remember seeing them as shadows."

"Yeah," Susan said. "That's right, and you feel like, *I can't hurt them [the parents]. They're already broken. I can't hurt them more.* So you sublimate it. I mean I numbed out, you know, psychologically and emotionally. So I think that's really important. If those children don't have a bucket to empty their grief into, if they mute themselves the way I did, the feelings are still going to be there."

Susan had put her finger on two key issues siblings face: how easy it is for children to become invisible, to exist in the shadow of their parents' grief. And the importance of giving the child a chance to express the turbulent inner emotions that follow the death of a sibling. Difficult as it may feel to talk about your child's death with your other children, you will be helping them in their healing process by doing so.

Depending on your child's age, there are a number of things you can do to help them express their feelings. With younger children you can use puppet play, storytelling, play with clay (building something and then smashing it can be a great release), or drawing. Talk about what your child is doing as he is making a picture or playing with puppets. Ask questions about the story he is telling. Expect to hear him express anger, sadness, and the fear that his sibling's death is a punishment because he somehow caused the death. You can reassure your child that he is safe, that you love him, that his sibling loved him, that he is not responsible for his sibling's death. Hugging him, having fun with him, and listening with empathy will help soothe him.

With older children, of course, you can have a conversation. Help them identify the feelings that are coming up for them, whether guilt, anger, responsibility, or regret. Survivor guilt is often a big issue for siblings. Susan said, "You feel guilty to be alive, guilty to be happy. You know this sense of inequity. I got to live and he had to die. And that's not fair." Siblings can also feel that the child who died gets elevated to the status of God, with photos all around or a shrine to her life. They end up feeling sidelined and alone in comparison. Or they may feel pressure to fill the deceased sibling's place, which can create confusion and anxiety.

To encourage conversation, you can say to your child, "I know what it is to have lost a child, but I don't know what it's like to have lost a sibling. Tell me what that's like." Whatever your child expresses, be prepared to listen. Reassure her that her feelings are normal, that they will not always be as strong as they are initially, and that you love your child and will be there for her when she needs you. And don't expect yourself to be perfect! I apologized to Fay and Andrew recently—thirty-seven years later!— for not being more attuned to their needs when Victor died. They graciously and lovingly accepted my apology.

If you want additional help for your child, you may be able to find a sibling support group in your area. These groups can help your child combat feelings of being different from her peers and alone in her grief. There are many

excellent books, for both children and parents, about dealing with sibling grief, and many online resources. Please
see the Suggested Reading at the back of this book for
more information.

. . .

WHAT IF MY CHILD DOESN'T WANT TO SPEAK OF HER BROTHER OR SISTER?

> My son refused to mention his sister's name. He acted
> as if he had never had that sister. My other daughter
> started wearing her sister's clothes and sleeping in her
> room. One ignored her and one wanted to become her.
> I was scared because I didn't feel I knew how to be helpful
> to my kids and I was afraid that they wouldn't be able to
> live with all that grief. Thank God there was a grief
> therapy group for siblings in our community. Just
> having a listener helped my kids a lot.
>
> —Leah, age forty, whose ten-year-old daughter had died
> in a swimming accident four years earlier

For several years after my son Victor's death, his younger
brother Andrew would listen quietly if we spoke of Victor
but would seldom say anything or tell stories about him.
I was worried about his silence, and wondered if it was
because of the depth of his trauma and shock. I attempted
at times to invite Andrew to speak about Victor but didn't
want to force the issue. I had to trust that he would speak
of Victor when he was ready, not when I thought he
should. Yet I worried because I had no clue how long that
would take.

Finally, after a few years had passed, Andrew seemed more open and did begin to speak of his brother again, referring to him as "Vic" and talking of the things they used to do together. Later, and with the help of a psychotherapist, Andrew was able to tell me that Victor's death was the hardest and saddest thing he'd ever had to deal with. I must admit I was grateful to hear that. Interestingly, when I spoke with Andrew recently, he said he was never silent about Victor, so I guess this is an example of remembering history differently! Our reality, whether past or present, belongs to each of us, and for each person it's unique. The same is true for our relationship to our deceased loved one.

Now Andrew reports that he feels close and loving with Victor. When he began dating his wife Sarah and introduced her to his family, he told her all about Victor. She recently told me that she feels Victor's loving presence in their home, and experiences her own spiritual connection with him. Sarah and Andrew's two young daughters know about Uncle Victor's life and death. In fact, they are named Violet and Ruby Valentina, names that begin with "V," after Victor.

I've also learned that it is not uncommon for children to wait to grieve until they are sure their parents are okay. It is painful for children to watch their parents' devastation, and they can feel helpless to make things better. They often wait to do their own grieving until after their parents have shown that they are not "falling apart." One mom asked her surviving daughter, six months after the death of her sister, "What do you want for your birthday?" Her daughter answered, "I just want you and dad to be happy again."

If a child backs away from conversation or gets angry or defensive when encouraged to share memories, it's important to let him take his time. Kids who "won't talk about it" are grieving—in their room, in the car, in the shower—just not with their parents. When your child seems more receptive, set an example by speaking about his brother or sister yourself, without expecting your child to add anything. Your deceased child is still part of the family. His absence is present, so bring him into the conversation when it feels right to do so. Talking about him can help relieve the tension of trying *not* to mention him. It can be a relief to everyone in your family.

• • •

WILL WE EVER GET BACK TO THE WAY WE WERE?

Everybody goes their separate ways. Used to be we did things together as a family. Whenever [my husband] Phil was home, we always had dinner together, or breakfast, or brunch.

—Kit, age fifty-six, whose seventeen-year-old daughter had died in an automobile accident three years and eight months earlier

This question can be one of the hardest to confront. The question itself carries such longing, and I am filled with compassion when parents speak these words. Behind the question lies the full measure of grief and devastation. The simple answer is no, you will not again have the family you had before. But there's no question you can once again

have a family that is whole, close, and functioning. Please
be reassured that this is the case, and that there are things
you can do to make a positive outcome more likely. Several things seem to be key.

In her article "Mourning Is a Family Affair," Esther
Gelcer writes that families cope with mourning most ef-
fectively when they share it. In my own research, I have
found this to be true. Families who were able to acknowledge the death of a child and to talk about it openly became closer. When the family can grieve collectively, they
are less negatively affected by the death. One mother I
spoke with, Bertha, said, "I think my children and I, as far
as being able to share the feelings, we didn't do it all the
time to the point of being excessive. But we did it. I realized that it was healthy to talk about it. I needed to talk
about it, and I found out that both children did, too."

Those families in which grieving was kept "under
wraps" became more distant. In these families, parents expressed a feeling that the family had in some ways grown
more separate as a result of the child's death. For some families, the impact on the other children and family life was
even worse. I spoke with one mother, Brenda, who said,
"Our family was falling apart. Our two boys were act-
ing out; they were taking drugs; they were drinking. Our
whole family was absolutely falling apart at the seams."

If your family experiences this kind of distress, I urge
you to seek family counseling with a qualified grief therapist who can help you to understand the feelings behind
destructive behaviors and to develop better ways to cope.
Even if you're simply concerned about increased feelings
of distance or the way a certain ease and joy has seeped

from your home, as air seeps from a balloon, counseling can help. Opening up the family conversation can provide a healthy vent for anger and resentment and increase closeness, empathy, and appreciation of what you still have together. What your family makes of your loss, how you understand it, has a lot to do with how you will move forward as a family.

Take stock of your positive feelings and of how you are nurturing a positive spirit within your family. Martha, one parent I asked to do this, said: "Suddenly, when one of your children dies, you realize how very precious they both were and the living one is. And I think I was more able to look at Luce as an individual and who she was and just accept her and love her the way she is." And Sharon said: "I'm more patient with them, much more patient with them, maybe too patient in that I go out of my way a lot to see that they get what I think they need. And I don't push."

And don't forget the tremendous value in making time to be together, for meals, a family movie, a day trip together. It may take effort at first, but the payoff is invaluable.

• • •

HOW CAN WE COPE WITH THE CHANGES IN OUR FAMILY?

Danny really felt and spoke out for the things that he felt were right and the things that weren't right and he

> courageously spoke to those, fearlessly. So Danny was
> into history and politics, so I didn't do it. I was into
> [being] social and piano and stuff like that, so he,
> you know, we just had our roles.
>
> —Susan L., age forty-nine, whose sixteen-year-old brother
> had died of medical mismanagement of a congenital
> condition thirty-six years earlier

When a family suffers the death of a child, it suffers much more than a singular loss. The family as it was previously, the familiar system, changes. Each member of the family plays a special role. With your child's death, roles that were established over many years shift. The family order changes. The child once in the middle might suddenly be the oldest. Or overnight, a younger child becomes the only child. Your children's familiar hierarchy is thrown out of balance and permanently disrupted.

After Victor's death, my middle son Andrew suddenly became the older son and the big brother to Fay, who had always been "Victor's baby sister." I asked Andrew if he felt the responsibility of being the older brother, and he said, "Yeah, yeah, I tried to. I tried to be supportive to Fay and show up for her." Andrew and Fay have definitely been there for each other during difficult times over the years. And interestingly, Susan L., quoted above, has an autistic son and has become a strong advocate for autistic families, speaking up courageously as her brother Danny might have!

Think about the role that your deceased child played with his or her siblings. Did they have fun together in a certain way? Did they read together and enjoy special toys or games? Did one look up to the other or feel overshadowed by that particular sibling? Answering these questions will give a clearer idea of what your surviving children have lost, and what you or other family members can do to soothe that loss. Recognizing what in particular has been lost for each child can allow you to find a creative way to fill the void. For instance, can you take your daughter to have her nails done with you since she no longer shares clothes or goes shopping with her sister? Can your family continue going to sporting events, vacations, and other family events that you had previously attended with your now deceased child? This kind of continuity can be reassuring for your whole family.

If you have a subsequent child after the death of a child, whether through conception or adoption, it's especially important to validate your new child as a unique and special individual. Loved and valued as he or she may be, it can be a challenge to lift the "replacement" burden from that child. It will help to see the subsequent child as the younger sibling of your deceased child, an individual in his or her own right, and to avoid comparisons.

Because families are complex, it is important to be patient and see how each member fares over a period of time. In the meantime, one of the best things you can do for your children is to show love and patience not only toward them but also toward your partner. If your children see you and your partner supporting and comforting each other, talking with kindness and compassion, they are far more likely to do the same.

• • •

AS A SINGLE PARENT, HOW CAN
I COPE WITH SUCH A LOSS?

Living seems like too much trouble. I just don't
have the energy for it. Most of the time I feel so
alone and so isolated. And yet there are lots of
people who care about me and who try.

—Madeline, age thirty-three, divorced, whose twelve-year-
old daughter had died of leukemia four months earlier

A single parent who loses a child carries a special burden.
To a certain extent, you are your own support system, and
if you have other children, you must provide emotional
support to them as well. If you lived alone with your child,
the quiet hours may seem empty and intolerable. The loneliness deepens your pain. If a substantial part of grieving is
acknowledging and giving expression to feelings about the
loss, then an empty room is all the more devastating. With
whom can you share your feelings? Who will provide the
comfort you need?

In a family-oriented culture, this aloneness can be especially alienating. Jill, whose seventeen-year-old son died
in an automobile accident two years and six months before
I interviewed her, lost her only son, and she and her husband divorced as well. This is how she expressed it: "I feel
in a way that I don't belong here anymore because I don't
have a right to a lot of things, or somehow I don't fit in because I don't have children and I don't have a husband, or
one or the other. So I feel my life has to be a little different
because of that. I have to find something very different to
do with my life instead of having a family. I just feel a little
bit out of it."

If you have similar feelings of aloneness, hopefully you have family members nearby who can give you the hugs and love you need, or a close friend. I encourage you to reach out to them and to spiritual leaders or guides, a grief counselor, or a therapist with specific training in grief. Even if your family or friends can't provide the support you need, please tell yourself that you do not need to go through the grief process alone.

A single father whose twenty-one-year-old son died in a car accident told me how his 12-step program gave him the fellowship and support to get through the tough and painful early days after his son's death. He told me that no matter what he was going through, there were people in his program who had experienced something similar. And he felt that the structure of his 12-step program offered him a guide for living one day at a time—or sometimes fifteen minutes at a time, or even five minutes at a time!

You can remind yourself that living with grief can be a lonely journey even when you have a partner or spouse because each person has a unique relationship with the child who died. Many people, single or not, feel alone in their grief. I like to remember the uplifting words of Jack Kornfield, founder of Spirit Rock Meditation Center in Northern California, which he shares in *A Lamp in the Darkness*: "One of the most difficult things about hard times is that we often feel that we are going through them alone. But we are not alone. In fact, your life itself is only possible because of the thousands of generations before you, survivors who have carried the lamp of humanity through difficult times from one generation to another. . . . And now, as you read these words, you can feel yourself as part of the stream of humanity walking together, finding ways to carry the lamp of wisdom and courage and compassion through difficult times."

• • •

WHAT DO I DO WITH THIS TREMENDOUS FEAR THAT SOMETHING WILL HAPPEN TO MY OTHER CHILD?

It doesn't occur to a mother that their child is going to
die except after one does. And then it occurs to the
mother all the time that possibly another one is going to.
I worry a lot about them because I know something else
can happen. And I wrestle with that all the time.

—Joan, age forty-nine, whose twenty-one-year-old son
had died in a sporting accident three years and four
months earlier

The new awareness of how fragile life can be often makes parents more fearful for their surviving children. The devastating awareness that you couldn't keep your child safe naturally creates concerns about your other children's safety. It's normal to find yourself worrying in this way. Research on PTSD is clear: We carry trauma in our body and brain. If you feel that there's been a reset in your stress and reactivity center, a structure in the brain called the amygdala, it's because there has been. Your amygdala will be triggered much more easily after a traumatic event than previously, creating stronger feelings of worry and fear.

For a long time after Victor died, if the doorbell rang unexpectedly I broke out in a panic and could not answer it. If one of my children was supposed to call and didn't, the panic rose up again. I remember waiting for Victor's phone call that Friday night, July 11, 1980. The call I never received. I still wonder why he didn't call when he said he would. The accident didn't occur until the next day. I will never have an answer to that question.

One night I was expecting a call from my son Andrew, and when the phone didn't ring, the worry escalated quickly. What if something happened? What if he died? My heart pounded. I want him to live a long life and be fulfilled. I want the pleasure of being a part of his life, his career. I want to witness his love for another, his marriage, my grandchildren. These worries could swamp me so easily. Then the phone rang and with it came a flood of relief.

These particular stresses are hard on everybody. One adult child I spoke with said, "I felt like I was living under a bell jar. I tried to be compassionate toward my mom, but she would lash out if I was a few minutes late or, to this day, don't text her back right away. I know now where it comes from, but it's a tough one!"

When you experience these moments of fear, your breathing is often shallow or irregular. This is the perfect time to do some of the deep-breathing exercises suggested earlier. If your breathing is shallow, concentrate on taking deep, easy breaths in and out. If you're breathing rapidly or hyperventilating, focus on slowing your breath. As you do so, you'll feel yourself calming down. In this more relaxed state, your racing mind will calm as well.

You might also want to repeat a soothing prayer or positive affirmation to yourself. An affirmation is simply a positive thought that, when repeated, can replace the negative thoughts in your head. You might say something like, "My child is at peace and cared for." When you repeat a phrase like this over and over, you'll find your worries are quieted. When I am frightened or upset, I often take slow, deep breaths and repeat to myself, "With compassion I breathe in love" on the in-breath and "With compassion I breathe out fear and worry" on the out-breath. These words soothe me. I encourage you to find the prayer or saying that works for you and keep it close to your heart.

· · ·

WE LOST OUR ONLY CHILD. HOW DO WE CREATE A FUTURE?

I just felt this utter destruction, because my daughter was such a part of me. I raised her, I taught her, and I shaped her. And I saw things developing that I didn't have, that I admired, that I wanted to see blossom. And I encouraged those things. And I felt all this beauty, this gorgeous flower, this magnificent thing that I created a lot of was destroyed.

—Bernice, age forty-nine, whose twenty-six-year-old daughter had died in an automobile accident five months earlier

The death of your child brings incredulity that you have outlived your child. But you also share a deep identity with your child that means the loss of your child is a loss of part of yourself. "When I lost my child, I lost myself," is an often-heard lament. Regardless of your child's age at death, you've lost a part of yourself that cannot be regenerated. When that child is your only child, the emptiness carries added layers of loss. You may wonder whom you can dream for when the one child on whom all your hopes were placed is suddenly gone. You may feel you've lost your link to the future, the wedding you won't dance at, the grandchildren you won't hold. This is why we say that grief after the death of a child is timeless. We grieve as we continually go through our own life stages. Every parent who has lost a child feels this pain, and it can be especially acute for the parent who lost an only child. Now your link to the future, that chain of lives that gives your life meaning, has been severed.

Mother's Day and Father's Day can be especially difficult, as you feel like outsiders, unable to join in the celebrations. What happens to your identity as a mother or father? A mother at a grief group I attended, whose only child died of an overdose of heroin, shared her pain at not having anyone to call her "Mom." We assured her she would always be her son's Mom, and encouraged her to hold him close in her heart and to always allow herself to hear his voice calling to her. Susan G., whose only child, Gabe, died at nineteen of an accidental overdose, put it this way: "My only child is physically gone. But I am still his mother and Steve, my husband, is still his father."

When I spoke with Pamela AP, whose seventeen-year-old daughter, Gabri, had taken her life two and a half years earlier, she talked about the urge to find another child to nurture. "At first I started trying to come up with all these things that I could do, like have a foster child or adopt, because I couldn't have any more kids and I still wanted to be a mother to a daughter." She began to cry. "I was going to miss all those things. But then I realized that nobody was going to be like Gabri and that it would just be chasing after something that I couldn't ever have again. And instead of then wanting to do things like that, I kind of just was reconciled to the fact that at the moment, it was best to not make those kinds of attempts to negotiate with God or the universe or whatever to survive the pain that way. I realized that I couldn't do that until I healed."

It may take time before you are ready to reinvest emotional energy in another relationship, but keep an open heart. Your child will never be replaced, but you can form new bonds that hold deep meaning. Your loss can be the inspiration for surprising new connections. Keep in mind the words of Mother Teresa: "The problem with the world is that we draw the circle of our family too small."

This may be a good time to turn to nature for comfort, especially those places of grandeur such as the ocean or the mountains, or some peaceful place that gives you the sense of being a small part of something bigger, something immortal. Here you can feel a connection with the vastness of life and the chains of life that go on despite our individual losses. The earth, which according to the *I Ching* "in its devotion carries all things, good and evil, without exception," is not only beautiful but sustaining. In spirit-nurturing places, you find a solace that can ease your heart and reassure you that the world goes on and your beloved child is still here, somewhere, a part of the grand design. The nature that made you and your child still holds you both in her hands, as much a part of the universe as a part of eternity.

• • •

WILL I EVER BE ABLE TO SEE OR HEAR ABOUT OTHER PEOPLE'S CHILDREN WITHOUT FEELING JEALOUS, ANGRY, OR RESENTFUL?

Why me? Every one of my friends still has their kids. God, why me? I was a good mother. I tried so hard, and he died anyway. I hope I don't get to be a nasty, bitter old lady.

—Martha, age forty-six, whose eighteen-year-old son had died in a bicycle accident eight months earlier

Cintia, whose eighteen-year-old daughter died from gang violence, said something I heard from a number of parents: "It is painful to see other mothers going shopping with their daughters, getting their nails done. Doing all the mother-daughter things we used to do. It hurts." The pain of your child's death can be reignited simply by the sight of other children, of what for you is missing. The parents of these children have what you do not, and that does hurt. The whirl of feelings evoked by the sight of a mother holding her daughter's hand or a father and son picking up some groceries at the market can be intense. Longing, anger, sadness, jealousy.

Another mother I spoke with, Gail, told me how she coped: "That's one thing I became very aware of, that I was jealous of that family, of the wholeness of that family. But then it hit me that day, too. That we can still be a whole family. In the physical way, we're only four. But this very moment we're creating a new family, sort of. And we're creating new memories."

This shift in thinking does not happen overnight. You won't suddenly find yourself free of jealousy. Longing will still tug at your heart. Yet if you allow your heart to open to the present, I promise you will find new gifts. You *are* making new memories, and forming a family in which your child is both present and not present.

In the meantime, you have every right to those feelings of sadness and jealousy. They make perfect sense. If you need to, give yourself permission to cry as much as you want, to change your mind about plans, to ask for what you want from others. Perhaps you can let others know what has triggered your pain and ask for their understanding. It's not always easy, but stating what you need can really help. Take some quiet time for yourself, for a soothing hot bath or a favorite walk. This is a time to be generous with yourself. Think of the words of Buddhist teacher Thich Nhat Hanh, who says in his book *Teachings on Love*, "take care of yourself. Your body needs you, your feelings need you, your perceptions need you. The wounded child in you needs you. Your suffering, your blocks of pain need you. Your deepest desire needs you to acknowledge it. Go home and be there for all these things. Practice mindful walking and mindful breathing. Do everything in mindfulness so you can really be there, so you can love."

• • •

WILL OUR MARRIAGE SURVIVE?

Ellen's death caused a lot of problems for us as a couple.
Just the grieving process does. It can cause such tension.
And it does affect your lovemaking. And it does affect

> your communication sometimes, because you
> clam up more. You don't share.
>
> —Camilla, age thirty-one, whose nine-day-old daughter had
> died from a congenital heart defect one year earlier

There's no question that your relationship with your partner is tested by the death of your child. It's not uncommon for one spouse, immersed in his own grief, to be emotionally unavailable, and for the other spouse to feel she isn't getting the emotional support she needs. Just as often, the sense of grief and loss is so strong that grieving parents frequently push their partners away. You may feel so consumed by your own emotions that little energy is left to deal with your relationship with your partner. You cannot reach out to each other, and your already intense grief is compounded by the strain in your marriage.

Over the more than three decades that I've counseled bereaved parents, I've seen over and over how vital it is that you continue to communicate with each other. All the research on parental bereavement underscores this idea. Psychologist Linda Edelstein, in her book *Maternal Bereavement: Coping with the Unexpected Death of a Child,* points out that the greatest difficulty for bereaved parents is their inability to discuss how they feel with each other. Coping, she said, involves "tolerating the separateness of the other and the loneliness of the experience without becoming permanently estranged."

Those couples who can work through this difficult time and stay together are usually those who share honest communication, however hard it may be. And make no mistake, it is hard work. It's not easy to give or take love and support when you're grieving, but it is possible. This still may not mean that you can get exactly what you want from each other. If you want to talk about your child, for example, and your husband or wife does not, perhaps you can find other supportive friends who will be the listeners you need. When your need to talk is met elsewhere, it might be easier for you to forgive your partner for having different needs.

Try to find ways to reach out to each other and keep your communication alive. Can you set aside a half hour at the end of the day, turn off the TV, and turn to each other? Try to listen to each other as if you are getting to know each other for the first time. In a way, you are doing exactly that. You and your partner are entering unfamiliar territory. You are trying to relearn a relationship and to share with each other in new ways. This is a time when both of you will discover new strengths as well as weaknesses. You will be discovering parts of each other that might be surprising, some you can admire and others that are hard to see, such as impatience, negativity, or heightened reactivity. You may not recognize yourself or your partner.

One mother said, "I screamed, cried, and moaned for an hour and a half, and he just held me and rocked me. And I'll never forget that day to the day I die. That he loved me enough to just let me do that." She saw in her husband a sensitivity and strength that deepened her love for him. The needs of grief are as intimate as the needs of love, and require the same commitment to honest communication.

● ● ●

WHAT IF MY PARTNER AND I ARE NOT IN SYNC?

> We never quite grieved at the same time, not on the
> same thing at the same time ever. When one of us was
> up, the other was down. When one was sad, depressed,
> and wanting to stay home, the other was feeling a
> spurt of energy to be social.
>
> —Dinah, age forty-three, whose twenty-four-year-old son
> had died in a construction accident fourteen months earlier

Most research on parental bereavement refers to the parents as if they were one person. However, each parent has a unique experience. The mother's experience is particular to a mother, has something in common with other mothers, and is different from the experience of the father. The same is true for the father's experience. This is an area that needs much more research and exploration. Based on stories and observation, it seems clear that the extent to which each spouse can respect and understand the other's differing needs may determine the future of the marriage. As one mother I interviewed said, "Everyone goes through it differently. And both Harold and I were trying to tell each other that we were wrong in the way we were doing it. But that wasn't true. We were both doing what was right for us as individuals. But we had to find that out later."

Because it is normal to feel separate and out-of-sync after the death of your child, the strain and distance in the relationship often grows. There may be differences in the need for emotional expression, with one partner crying a great deal or wanting to talk a lot about their child and the other less inclined to express grief in those ways. Justin, whose fifteen-year-old daughter died of medical misman-agement, reflected on the differences between him and his wife: "I mean, Myrna is in constant pain and she cries a lot and she's just feeling her feelings all the time. And I, when I get involved in something I'm able to kind of focus on that; live in the moment, so to speak. I watch some-thing on TV or go to a movie, I'm paying attention to the movie. So I'm able to kind of get a break from things. I think I'm just very different that way from Myrna."

Differences in whether emotions are openly expressed or kept under control can be especially difficult. One part-ner may feel resentful of the other for being able to ap-pear okay in the face of their tragedy, to go to work and continue to function. There are likely to be differences in the level of intensity or duration of your grieving, in your need for emotional comfort, in levels of fatigue. Any of these differences can lead to increased anger and blame toward each other and can drive a painful wedge between you at a time when you most need each other's compassion and love. You may feel helpless to make things better and confused about how best to support each other.

At this extraordinary time of loss, another extraordi-nary effort is needed. Those couples who are able to re-main committed and supportive of each other are those who can understand the need to accept, even value, their differences. Justin went on to say, "But I think the biggest challenge, you know, is it's probably unlikely that both people will be grieving the same way, and you know, you just have to recognize that. And so you need to accept that and not think there's something wrong with them."

When you can suspend judgment, remain patient, be open to listening, and not expect your partner to be like you, you will be more likely to turn toward each other rather than away and to strengthen and reaffirm your bond. Find something positive to say to each other at least once a day, something your partner has said or done that you appreciate. And if you feel unable to reach out to each other in positive ways, I encourage you, when you're ready, to find a skilled grief therapist who can help.

The question is: What do we lack most when we are grieving and suffering? Compassion. Compassion for all parts of ourselves, even the parts that feel unlovable and unacceptable. Compassion for who we are and who we are not. Compassion toward our partner who is confused and hurting and perhaps feeling his or her own inadequacies. This largeness of heart will go a long way toward helping you both to heal.

• • •

WHAT ARE THE SPECIAL
ISSUES FATHERS FACE?

Bonnie owns a business but it's been a part-time income, so I was the breadwinner. And I felt that pressure of having to go back to work and support your family when it's the last thing on earth you have any interest in doing, you know, trying to get the strength to be able to go and perform. I'm in sales, and that was very tough.

—Alan, age fifty-four, whose eighteen-year-old son had died in a car accident nine years earlier

Fathers often describe how they struggle after the loss of a child because the focus is on taking care of their wives and families rather than on taking care of themselves. Alan, whose eighteen-year-old son had died in a car accident, was surprised by the response of his colleagues at work. "When I returned to work after our son died, colleagues asked me how my wife was doing. Didn't they know that I, too, had lost a child? No one asked how I was doing." He felt invisible in his grief compared to his wife.

Our society gives women permission to cry, act out grief, and be open and honest with feelings. Men, however, are taught to be in control and keep their feelings to themselves. The messages to "hold it together" or "get on with life" can be particularly strong for men. One father I spoke with made a comment that was not unusual: "For a long time I've been dealing with some of the effects of my upbringing where being emotional is not supported. I was raised in this situation where feelings were suppressed."

It's not uncommon for a man to walk away when his wife starts to cry. He may distance himself because he feels uncomfortable or because he doesn't know what to say to help his wife feel better. Seeing her tears, he may fear that his wife will be stuck in her grief forever, and will want her to stop talking about her grief or want her to get up and return to her normal activities. These are not signs of a lack of caring, but a different way of coping.

Often men quickly retreat into work and hobbies. It may seem uncaring and cold, but these behaviors may simply reflect a more "male" model of coping that allows the bereaved to take a break from mourning. There's nothing wrong with that! Jim's thirty-four-year-old daughter died

unexpectedly in a running accident. He said, "My experience is, men and women take loss differently. And it's been
harder on my wife. You know, I find ways to not have to
think about it."

I have no doubt that grief is deep and long-lasting for
men as well as women, and men need the same opportunity to grieve. With their partner's love and encouragement, men often can be more open than they were
originally taught to be. If so, everyone will benefit from
that openness. One father whose daughter died a year and
two months earlier told me recently that in the privacy
of his own study, when he wants to express his grief, he
listens to his daughter's playlist of music and begins to sob
and grieve. He feels close to her in these moments, and
feels better afterward.

Since tension, anger, guilt, grief—our whole spectrum
of emotion—reside in the body, it makes sense that powerful emotions can be released through the body and various
body practices. As a dance/movement therapist, I always
encourage grieving parents to find ways to express their
emotions through movement, whether free-style dancing, various yoga and breathing exercises, or even bang-
ing drums. It's important to find healthy, physical ways
to release anger, sadness, and grief, such as taking a hike,
running, playing a sport, hurling rocks into the ocean, ripping a telephone book to shreds—anything that will serve
as a safe release. A bereaved father described to me how
swimming was the one thing that provided relief for him
initially. "Something about the act of swimming, or water,
or putting my head underwater or something. That's the
only time I can now remember I got any relief at all."

Try this: When you and your partner feel able, in a quiet moment, ask each other how your family of origin handled difficult emotions. Did they talk about them openly? Keep them to themselves? When someone you knew was going through a hard time, were you able to talk with other family members about what was going on? Did the men and women in your family express their emotions differently? How so? These conversations can be revealing and help you understand the differences in expectations and experience that you each bring to your marriage.

• • •

HOW CAN WE FEEL SEXUAL NOW?

Lovemaking was practically nonexistent, much less frequent. It's like that part of me shut down. And not because it was anything unpleasant. It was just knowing you're so different from the person you used to be. You can't go back to doing things the way you used to do them. It's just not the same.

—Joyce, age forty, whose thirteen-year-old son had died in a skiing accident three years and four months earlier

Sexuality is an intense subject anytime, especially when linked with grief. Putting those two words in the same sentence can seem unnatural. Do you feel guilty having sex, or even fear that your child's spirit is watching you? Do you cry silently while trying to be there for your partner? Are you fearful this part of your relationship will die or be permanently altered? You are not alone.

Sexual expression and need are areas in which being out-of-sync can bring additional pain. The energy in your marriage may suddenly diminish or disappear altogether, and this can include your feelings of sexual desire. Either of you may have sexual needs that are not being met. You might want to be held when your partner doesn't seem to be available or willing. You might feel lonely because you sense your partner is not emotionally present. You might also want to feel close without being sexual. Some parents find sex emotionally painful, while others believe that, although sex at first is strained, it is an important way to achieve closeness and support.

Here is how Connie and Brad, whose seventeen-year-old son had been shot six years earlier, expressed their differences. Connie said, "I remember being very numb, and so I wanted Brad to hold me. I needed to be hugged because I needed to feel safe, so I knew that I wasn't going to fall through the earth. But I didn't necessarily want to make love. I just, I needed to be comforted."

And Brad: "That first year was such a blur that like all you felt was pain. But I do know, for me as a man, love-making is a way of being comforted or a way of being loved. You know, that's how men understand love is through sex. And so for me, I probably wanted to make love more than normal as a way to either stay connected or feel love or to feel comforted or to somehow lessen the pain in some way."

Problems arise when partners are in disagreement about sexual behavior, especially when one partner is shocked or angered by the other's sex drive. Some parents report a rise in sexual activity immediately after their child's death. One mother said, "Initially after Danny died, within a week we became like sex fiends. It was like, 'We are alive' kind of thing. We became very needy. Now we have very little sexual desire. Both of us just declined drastically. And that bothers me, too." This roller coaster of emotions and sexuality can be disconcerting.

Whatever is true for you, discuss it, explore it together. Set aside a time each week to reach out to each other and talk honestly. Remind yourself: whatever you feel, it is right for you in this moment. This is another area where respecting each other's differences is so important. There is no right or wrong. What matters is that you be open with your partner about what you want or need.

• • •

How can we get through the holidays?

This year will be the third Christmas without him. And in some ways this is harder than the other two. The first one I was kind of in shock and going to be strong. The second I was still strong. And now it's really hit home. And all of a sudden I see things and find myself crying.

—Sonya, age forty-one, whose sixteen-year-old son had died in a fall three years and two months earlier

One December I saw in my therapy practice the mother of a twenty-one-year-old young woman who had died suddenly from a virus two years earlier. The mother was struggling to get through the holidays. She and her husband had decided not to put up a Christmas tree or decorate their house with lights. "Why should we act like we are feeling festive and celebrating," she said, "when we are not? If people pass our house and see lights they will think we are 'back to normal' and we're not. Holidays are for other people, not for us." I saw the tears pooling in her eyes and felt such compassion for her. "I wish I could create magic," I said to her, "and take your hurt away and bring your child back." I wish, I wish, I wish.

If the difficulties surrounding the holidays feel insurmountable, remember that you are in charge of what you choose to do. If, like the mother above, you don't want to celebrate, honor your instincts. You have every right to do what feels right in your heart at this moment. And also know that through some mystery, with time, you can and will feel a shift. There will come a time when you can make new memories and these days will not be filled with dread.

Some families find that getting away helps them cope, whether to a nearby campground where you can sit beneath the trees, or to some distant place. Peggi, whose nineteen-year-old son Jordan died by suicide at the end of his freshman year in college, wanted to surround herself with something completely new to divert herself from the intensity of her grief. "Eight months after Jordan's death, Christmas loomed. Something inside of me knew I could not stay at home that first Christmas. I had no idea where to go. I just had to leave. My husband, Jeff, came up with a plan to travel to the Atacama Desert in northern Chili. The trip was difficult but also healing. The culture was so different. Christmas festivities were subdued and it was not the wildly celebratory event it seems to have become in the U.S. This dramatic change in environment helped us." Whatever you need to do, believe in yourself and your

ability to find the right way to manage. This is a time to
think creatively and to stay attuned to your heart.

When the time is right, you might try talking with
your family about how you can celebrate in a way that
includes and honors your child. Can you, as a family, do
some artwork that will commemorate and include your
child? Or design a ritual, such as singing a song together
that your child particularly liked, or lighting a circle of
candles for each family member? Did she have favorite
holiday decorations that you can display as she would like?
Or a joke that always made you laugh? This is a time to be
creative, to respond from the heart, and to feel the healing
energy that comes from this expression of love. And if you
or your family are not ready for these changes, you can
still have your own private ritual that will allow you to
remember and feel close to your child.

• • •

How do I share my feelings with others?

Generally I cry alone. It doesn't seem to be accepted
any more. People look upon it as regression. You're
still not getting on with it. I think it's a part of my life
and will always be. But it's not easy. And I resent
sometimes that I go on and I'm having a good time,
and people probably think, "Isn't that nice—they've
forgotten all about it." But I haven't forgotten.

—Daisy, age forty-six, whose sixteen-year-old son had died
in a motorcycle accident four years and two months earlier

Any parent whose child has died understands how difficult it is to share their tumult of emotions with friends, family, or the world at large. Most people experiencing grief know the feeling of having other people back away when they begin to talk about their grief and pain. I interviewed a father recently who said a friend of his told him, "I can't hear about your son. It's too painful for me. Please don't talk to me about it." Who can listen to our feelings? To whom can we say, "I'm scared," "I feel like I'm going crazy," or "I can't stand this anymore"?

These are difficult questions, and there is no right answer. Sharing grief, especially in a culture that promotes stoicism and "bucking up," is a tricky undertaking. I remember the difficulties of doing everyday, mundane tasks, such as going to the grocery store or bank. People greet you with, "How are you today?" or say, "Have a good day." My response, rather than lie, was to say, "Some days are better than others." If they began chatting about something that I couldn't bear to hear, I said simply, "It's too painful for me to hear this today."

We can cut short our interactions with strangers, but most people need at least one place where they can be open and honest about their grief. This is one reason joining a group for bereaved parents can be so helpful. Here you're in the company of others who have been through the fire as you have and who "smell the smoke on each other," as one father put it so powerfully. Other bereaved parents are more likely to understand from a piercing depth the emotions you're expressing, and to be able to hear the full honesty of what you're experiencing. Finding an experienced grief counselor is another good option. In the safety of a counseling session, you can express your most uncensored feelings and feel listened to and heard.

Some people find it helpful to write down those feelings that are hard to share. You can write on the computer or buy or make a special journal to hold your thoughts. Because the journal is yours alone, the form your writing takes does not matter. Experiment with it, and take the time to discover how and when you want to write. If you want to write directly to your child, do so. If you want to write fragments, or snatches of poetry, or letters to other family members, do what feels right for you. When you write about your feelings, you have a better chance of sorting them out. For example, you may harbor intense anger toward someone who was involved in your child's death. Writing about that anger may show you how to confront that person and give you the courage to do so. Or it may enable you to find your own peace with those feelings. You may find you no longer need to share as much with people who are not able to hear what you express. All of this discovery is part of the process of healing.

• • •

WHAT DO I DO WITH THESE FEELINGS OF LONELINESS OR SEPARATION, THE FEELING THAT NO ONE ELSE IN THE FAMILY UNDERSTANDS?

I find it difficult to talk to my sisters and brother, my immediate family. It's as though it never happened. They never mention Mack. They're afraid to say

anything because if they do, it may bring tears to my
eyes and they feel they've hurt me when really I haven't
been hurt. I really wish my family would accept it and
was able to talk. It would probably help me.

—Rita, age forty-seven, whose twenty-five-year-old son
had died from an aneurysm one year earlier

Loneliness within your own family is especially painful, since this is where you expect to be nurtured. When
siblings, parents, or partners seem unable to understand
or listen to your grief, you feel betrayed. One bereaved
mother related how she felt confused and hurt when her
sister wasn't there for her as she would have expected. "I
had people that I thought were my closest, like my sister, I
thought she was my closest friend. She has not called me.
I haven't heard from her. I mean she sends me little texts
and cards and things, but it's been all this time and she
never comes over."

I have heard so many stories like this, involving both
friends and family of the bereaved. Another mother, Joan,
made a typical comment: "When the mention of my
child's name stops the conversation, the loneliness comes
back. People get tired of listening, as you well know, and
'Oh my God, don't bring that up, you'll depress everybody.' Even our own family will say that sometimes." Another bereaved mother, Laurie, tells this story: "Recently
the fellows said [to her husband], 'Well, how's Laurie doing?' And Frank said, 'Well, she's fine.' And they said,
'You know, we've been waiting for her to get over her
grief.' And I said to Frank, 'Well, tell them to wait another
hundred years, then.' I mean, it's not going to happen. But

to wait, that's ridiculous. In other words, they don't want to deal with it."

You probably have your own stories to tell. If you have felt lonely and frustrated when family or friends don't seem to understand your experience of loss or the grief process, finding even one friend or family member who does understand and who can listen empathetically is especially important. My mentor and teacher June Singer, whose only child Judy died in a car accident, created what she called her "intentional family," a group of people she felt close to and with whom she could speak honestly. I was lucky to be a part of that intentional family, and found comfort among people who could hear anything I needed to express.

If creating such a group is possible for you, I urge you to do so. Or you can join a ready-made bereavement support group through a local chapter of The Compassionate Friends—there are 700 local chapters across the United States. For more information, check the Resource List in the back of this book. Sharing your feelings with other bereaved parents is a good way to help you feel less alone in this new unfamiliar world, the strange world one enters after a child dies. No two people experience grief and loss in precisely the same way, but in the company of others who have walked the path you are walking, you'll be more likely to feel connected and understood. Then, hopefully, it will be easier to accept the limits to what you can expect from other family members and friends.

• • •

How do I handle my parents' or other family members' different ideas about grieving?

> I got mad at my mother. My husband got mad at his mother, his sister, and his cousin. We've had a bunch of upsets with family and friends over death. And things my mother-in-law will say now just absolutely infuriate me. One day I'm going to tell her. I haven't yet.
>
> —Lu, age forty-one, whose seventeen-year-old son had died in an auto accident six years earlier

It's important not to forget the grandparents, aunts and uncles, and other extended family. They are part of the family and will experience the loss of their grandchild or niece or nephew intensely. For grandparents, grief has two dimensions: they experience the devastating death of a grandchild and must watch their own child suffer pains that cannot be erased. One grandfather I spoke with described, with tears in his eyes, how difficult it is to witness his daughter's and son-in-law's pain at the loss of their child: "What makes me the saddest is knowing that what I am going through, they are going through 1,000 times more. And I know that even though I want to, I can't make it better for them." Feelings of helplessness, of not being able to make things right for their own child, can make the tragic loss of a grandchild doubly painful. Whether you have a close relationship with your parents and turn to them in difficult times, or have a complicated relationship with them, they cannot make this tragedy go away.

When my father talked about Victor, he frequently cried and said it was the worst thing that had ever happened. He always mentioned how loving and attentive Victor was to him. He said he felt terribly guilty that he hadn't gone to Yosemite with Victor when Victor asked him to. Instead Victor had gone with a boy he hardly knew. Would Victor still be alive if his grandfather had gone with him? These questions haunted us all. I knew how deeply both my parents grieved, and I tried to understand that we were all affected and touched by his death, each in our own way.

After Victor died, my mother removed all photos of him from the table where she kept the family pictures. I felt hurt and asked her why she did that. She explained that it was too painful to see his picture every day. She needed to protect herself from the pain, and I wondered if she were also trying not to show her feelings and be vulnerable in front of others. I realized that she had a right to do what she needed to do.

If your parents don't want to talk and you do, or if they feel you're spending too much time in grief, or if your grieving styles conflict in any way, I encourage you to be understanding of them. Try to accept that they are struggling with their own difficult feelings and to give them room to manage those feelings in the way that is right for them. You can find what you need from others who aren't overwhelmed with the same conflicts and emotions as your parents. You can be clear about what you need while accepting the idea that your parents or other family members may not be the ones to meet those needs. And you may be surprised when at a later time you're able to talk with your family more honestly about this painful time in your lives.

PART 3

ONE YEAR AND BEYOND: WHERE AM I NOW?

MY STORY: REMEMBERING VICTOR

One-year anniversary, July 12, 1981, Atherton, California

Last night at dark, my husband and I lit a Yahrzeit memorial candle for Victor and said our silent prayers to keep him safe and at peace. I have been dreading this day and just want to get through it. I'm not sure I can get through any more years like the last one. I wonder if I will begin to feel some relief from the burning in the pit of my stomach and the excruciating torture of grief. I have noticed moments recently when for a brief time I didn't feel my shattered heart, moments of feeling almost normal. Being able to concentrate on things other than Victor. But I still don't recognize myself in the mirror. I still look into my eyes and don't know who I am seeing. Not me. It seems like only minutes since Victor died and an eternity.

Fay and Andrew are away at their summer activities, so this afternoon, my husband, David, and I drive to the area in the Palo Alto hills where, not long after Victor's cremation, we had sprinkled his ashes from the shoebox-sized container we were given. We take a walk on a tree-shaded dirt path to honor Victor's love of the outdoors. As we breathe in the warm summer air and pine smells, we share stories about Victor's birth, babyhood, and teenage years.

I'm amazed at how much, as parents, we carry inside us. The inner world of parents holds all the history, all the details of their children's birth and life. We carry them in our heads, in our hearts, in the tissues of our cells. Many of these memories will go with us to our graves. Some we try to forget, and others we pray never to forget.

I was all of twenty-two when Victor was born. In some ways we grew up together. My husband and I fumbled along at learning how to be parents while growing up ourselves. I always felt that Victor and I were on some deep level soul mates. We could glance at each other across the table and understand what was being expressed without speaking. We shared the same sensitivities and sense of humor. We understood each other in a way that went beyond our relationship as mother and son. We seemed to live in the same type of psyche or spiritual world. When he died I lost not only a son but a close, intimate friend.

When I think of Victor, I see his smiling, dimpled face and his compassionate, warm eyes. His special connection while hugging, his natural handsomeness, his light-brown curly hair that he let grow longer for a while. His love of handmade boots. It seems weird to be describing his "physical body" because I don't really think of him in a physical body now. A body seems so limiting for his hugeness and for the vastness of his spirit. And yet it is that physical connection that I miss so much. The hugs, the glances, the voice. My Victor.

He didn't always look happy. Sometimes he looked sad or distant. Life wasn't always easy for Victor. He had dyslexia, probably ADHD, and struggled with school. My husband's work involved traveling; we moved fourteen times in the first twelve years of our marriage. Victor's first grade was a Spanish-speaking class in Mexico, a difficult situation for a learning-disabled child. His self-esteem was affected by his difficulties in school. Physical activities came more easily to him, and he loved soccer and skiing. He could work magic with his hands and fix almost everything and never read directions. Children and older people were drawn to him, and he always felt like one of those "old souls" to me. He had a snake tank in his room and loved his snakes. I wonder if Victor knew that snakes are a symbol of transformation and healing.

Quite often he was a handful. Victor was always running. Even as a baby when he crawled, he crawled fast. When he got his first red fire engine for his second birthday, he got in it and ran immediately over the curb into the street before I could stop him. He never seemed to know how to stop at street corners or obey signs that said, "Don't go any farther than this point." He was always going faster than I thought safe. When he learned to drive, he got speeding tickets. I hoped he would learn from his mistakes and that he would survive it all. There were times we were convinced he was doing drugs, maybe even selling. Teens we didn't know would come to our door. We worried about some of the friends he hung out with and whether he would get into college. He loved the Grateful Dead and hitchhiked to a few of their concerts. His father and I didn't approve, but we didn't have much influence in this respect. His favorite song, ironically, was the Grateful Dead's "Fire on the Mountain."

One week before Victor died, his father and I were in the kitchen. I said, my fists closed as if holding on to reins, "I feel as if I've been holding Victor back and trying to keep him safe ever since he was born. Sometimes I feel as if we have been keeping him alive all these years. He is almost eighteen years old." I unfolded my hands. "It's up to him and God now."

A few days later, my friend Kay came for dinner and a swim. It was a breezy California evening. As we soaked in my bubbling Jacuzzi, I admitted to Kay that even though we had been friends for many years and openly discussed our lives and professions, there was something I had heard about but was shy to discuss with her. The death of her daughter was something I didn't feel comfortable bringing up because I didn't want to cause her pain or discomfort. Yet I felt compelled to talk with her about it. She warmly encouraged me to ask her anything, and she began telling the story of how her teenage daughter had burned to death in a fire seven years earlier.

I remember looking at this attractive, warm, loving, wise woman and wondering how she had survived. I didn't think I could, if something like that happened to my child. It would be unbearable. I thought she must have some inner strength or secret gained from living through such a catastrophic trauma. I would not want to gain strength that way. It was beyond my imagination. I counted my blessings.

Later that evening, as we went into the house, Victor called out from his bedroom, asking us to keep him company while he packed for his trip to Yosemite the next day. Kay and I sat on his waterbed and chatted with him while he stuffed clothes and a journal into his red backpack. He looked strikingly handsome and self-confident. That night he was happy, excited, and talkative. He was a very proud high school graduate of two weeks and looking forward to becoming "The Big 18" in another week.

The next day he left for Yosemite with a boy he barely knew. He had asked his grandfather to go to Yosemite with him and then me, but neither of us felt we could. I dropped him off at the corner of Highway 280. I didn't like him hitchhiking to Yosemite, but he insisted that was the only way to go this time.

"Be careful, Honey," I reminded him. "I love you." I blew him a kiss.

"Oh, Mom, I'll be careful. Don't worry. I don't want to die. I love you too." He smiled.

Five days later Victor was dead. I have often wondered why Kay and I had finally talked about her child's death on that evening, before we visited with Victor in his room. Had I had a premonition?

David and I stand quietly, looking up through tree branches at the blue sky above, before heading back to our car. I feel my heart pounding. I am light-headed. A surge of energy races through my chest. The memory of being in Victor's room that night with my friend Kay, watching Victor pack, is as clear as if it was yesterday. How I wish, with all my heart and from the depths of my soul, that I could go back to that night and stop the clock.

Then I remember my dream, the soothing, reassuring dream I had last night. As the one-year anniversary approached, I had hoped and prayed for a sign from Victor. I know this dream was that sign: I'm in a beautiful large meadow of high green grass and bright orange and red poppies when suddenly a large, scary, foreboding man appears, his outstretched arms and legs blocking the sun. In a loud voice he proclaims: "Watch! I can make the sun stop shining." I start smiling and then laughing and say to him, "You can block the sun's rays from shining on me, but you will *never* stop the *son* from shining."

. . .

How can I handle the first anniversary?

As I got close to the anniversary, I got scared to death. I was afraid I'd totally freak out, that I'd go crazy and never come back. I was glad someone else acknowledged the anniversary and remembered, and I felt myself almost wanting to tell people. I'm recognizing that the year without her is like coming full circle, and I need to live with it.

—Lolly, age forty, whose eighteen-year-old daughter had died in an automobile accident one year earlier

The first anniversary of your child's death is a significant milestone. In many cultures, the official end of publicly mourning a death comes one year after the event. Often this day is observed with some outward gesture, such as a change in clothing from black to everyday colors or a feast to remember the dead and signal your return to the normalcy of life. These rituals do not mean grief is over nor that, at one year after your child's death, your grief should be gone. It's simply a calendar mark that is culturally observed but that can carry deep inner meaning. You have now gone through each season for the first time without your child, the first Thanksgiving, the first Chanukah or Christmas, the first New Year's Eve, winter, spring, summer, fall.

Probably you anticipated the day with mixed emotions, the most prominent of which might well be fear. You might fear that you will not bear up under the strain or even that you may not survive this dreaded time. You fear the memories that will come rushing back, and a new surge of the emotions that have been so overwhelming. Yet you may be surprised at how the day turns out. One mother said, "It was like I'd had twenty pounds of sandbag on my shoulder that year. And for some reason, that day I woke up and the sandbag was gone."

Wherever you are in your own grieving process, marking this first year is important for your onward journey. Please give yourself some special time and do what your heart wants. If you want to stay in your room with the shades down, please do. If you want to run a marathon with friends to raise money for a scholarship in your child's honor, go for it! Or perhaps you prefer to spend your own quiet time with your child, holding her in your heart, expressing your love for her, writing her a letter, or talking to her. Whether you want to spend this anniversary with friends or family, by yourself, doing something for others, or taking a walk in nature, I encourage you to honor what feels right for you. However you experience and mark this passage, you might simply note that you have just lived through one year of the unbearable. A year ago, as you were dealing with the first terrible shock of your child's death, you probably would have thought even this would be impossible.

Having survived the first year following your child's death, please acknowledge yourself for surviving. Only you know the emotions, events, and changes that have taken place in this first year. And only you know the strength it has taken to find a path through the maze of grief.

• • •

Who am I now?

You look in the mirror; you're not the same anymore.
The air you breathe isn't the same anymore. The way
you are isn't the same anymore.

—Beryl, age fifty-one, whose twenty-eight-year-old son
had died in a motorcycle accident one year and four
months earlier

Yes, you are changing. It is not just your imagination, nor that of your friends and family. The death of a child assures that you will change. It makes you look at the world and at life and death in a new way. Bereaved parents—indeed, anyone who has suffered devastating loss—often talk about a "before" and "after": the life you had before and the life you have after. Sonya, whose sixteen-year-old son had died in a fall three years and two months earlier, says, "I still relate almost everything to before and after Steve's death. Mother will say, 'Remember when such and such happened,' and I immediately know if it's before or after." Death provides a stark divide. It is a dividing line through your life and through who you are as a person.

At the one-year mark, your new self, the mother or father who has suffered the death of a child, is no longer a stranger to you whose ways are unpredictable and wild. You are becoming familiar with yourself as a parent who has lost his or her child. No matter how much time passes, there is always that reminder, whether it is piercingly sharp or naggingly dull, that a death has occurred and your child is missing from your life. You can never go forward as if your child's death had not happened.

You may be carrying around an anger that is unfamiliar to you. Or your heightened awareness of loss and life's fragility may make you more fearful or guarded. You may feel less ready to open yourself emotionally, and this can affect your ability to love. The past year may have dulled those loving parts of you, which is a natural, protective reaction. Take heart in knowing that this is usually temporary, and that you will gradually feel your loving, more open self reemerging. You may feel this already. If you are asking, "Really?" the answer is "Yes."

Other changes are more positive. You may feel that the excruciating, painful longing for your child is becoming more tolerable. Or you might have done something recently that would have been impossible only months before, such as visit with a friend with genuine pleasure, without feeling you're only going through the motions. You might have a new sense that you can assert your needs and stand up for yourself in ways you once found difficult. Perhaps you now have a greater sense of the value of your life, or you are less willing to waste time on tasks that have no meaning for you. One mother I spoke with said, "I think I've changed my priorities, what's really important to me. I spend more time doing the things I want to. Sometimes I have this feeling, 'I'm going to do this because I really want to.' It's like taking care of me."

Think back over the last weeks and months and ask yourself what has changed for you. What new feelings do you have? What are you doing now that you couldn't have done six months ago? What has surprised you? Give yourself credit for the ways you are coping and getting stronger, and compassion for the ways that difficult feelings still walk with you through your days.

• • •

EVERYONE EXPECTS ME TO BE "BETTER" AFTER A YEAR, BUT WHAT IF I DON'T FEEL BETTER?

Generally, I cry alone. My grief doesn't seem to be accepted anymore. "You're still not getting on with it," they'll say. I think it's part of my life and always will be. Friends probably think, "Isn't that nice? She's forgotten all about it." But I haven't forgotten.

—Kit, age fifty-six, whose seventeen-year-old daughter had died in an automobile accident three years and eight months earlier

A year is not really a long time, even if it has sometimes felt like the longest year of your life. It takes time to recover from the shock you have undergone, probably more time than you expected. Certainly more time than you want. According to the book *Devastating Losses*, studies on parental grief have shown that it can take three to five years to find a "new normal" after the death of a child, and that after one year many parents still experience higher-than-average levels of emotional distress and post-traumatic stress, sleep disturbance, anxiety, physical ailments, anger, self-reproach, and memory problems. In fact, the second year for some parents can be harder because there's not as much shock to protect you, or not as much focus on practical matters like planning a service or establishing a memorial, so you may feel the loss and the pain more now. The finality of your loss may only be beginning to sink in.

That time when you feel more healed doesn't arrive in a neat package or happen along a straight path without any obstacles or bends in the road. Healing occurs haphazardly and irregularly. You cannot force the pace. Your inner being has its own timetable, and even if you feel frustration or sometimes despair, these feelings will resolve themselves eventually.

In the first shock and hurt of your loss, probably everyone allowed you to grieve as you wished. Those people may have different ideas for you as time passes. They may want you to stop grieving, to act as if everything is now as it was before. Marti's experience is not unusual: "When Lance died I was surrounded by people, friends and family and the community. And then all of the sudden it was gone. And you're alone and nobody wants to come. They don't want to sit with your grief. And there were a few people that would sit in the fire with me, but not many."

Be kind to yourself and, if necessary, tell others who think you should be healed, "This is a personal journey and only I know what it feels like." Most people find grief confusing, mysterious, and often hard to cope with. It is very likely that people who have not suffered the death of a child will not truly understand your own passage through grief, nor comprehend its complexity and constancy in your life.

That does not make them wrong. They simply do not know what you know. Writer Iris Murdoch expressed this feeling succinctly: "Bereavement is a darkness impenetrable to the imagination of the unbereaved." Many grieving parents continue to find that support groups are a good place to find mutual understanding. Talking with other bereaved parents provides empathy, comfort, and a view into the many ways parents navigate this journey.

• • •

SHOULD I STILL BE FEELING THIS SAD?

> I don't have the real excitement, drive, and push that I had before. I guess I was a wonder woman. I had the feeling that I could conquer anything. I was sure of myself. I don't feel that good about myself. I don't have the interest to do the things I should be doing.
>
> —Rita, age forty-seven, whose twenty-five-year-old son had died of an aneurysm one year earlier

It is unlikely that you will suddenly wake up and no longer feel sad. Sadness is likely to be your companion, on and off, in an ongoing way. Most parents speak of experiencing moments of sadness for the rest of their lives. Sadness and

missing our children become a natural and expected part
of life that, miraculously, we learn to live with. Yet you
may recognize now that sadness does not always take the
outward forms, like weeping or wanting to scream. Those
moments may still well up and take you by surprise. But
there will be longer periods between the weeping, more
times when you engage in your daily life without feeling
swept by the most acute pain.

I remember, in the years after Victor died, reading
a book called *Motherhood and Mourning* by psychologists
Larry Peppers and Ronald Knapp about perinatal death,
and coming across their concept of "shadow grief," by
which they meant grief that is never fully resolved. Their
words caught my attention. Shadow grief is felt as a dull
ache in the background of one's feelings that remains fairly
constant and that, on certain occasions, comes bubbling
to the surface, sometimes in the form of tears, sometimes
not, but always accompanied by sadness and a mild sense
of anxiety. This made such sense to me. It was a relief to
understand that, as the years go on, an undercurrent of
grief is not unusual and does not signal that something is
wrong.

Psychologist and researcher Linda Edelstein is one of
many who question whether the word "completed" is
even applicable to parental grief. She and other researchers have described mourning as full of conflict and complex oscillation between resolution and regression. In her
book *Maternal Bereavement* she writes, "The struggles are
not fought and won, but faced again and again. Progress
is seen as the conflicts become less frequent, less intense,
of shorter duration, and easier to understand." To expect a

resolution or an end point to grief is to misunderstand the nature of grief.

Even a year after Victor's death, I had days when the overwhelming loss lurked in the background, ready to pounce. The excruciating pain changes over time to a dull ache, but it doesn't disappear. Even though I told myself, during this time, what I tell my clients—"be patient with yourself; have compassion; it's not what happens to you in life, but what you do with it"—I struggled to accept my own advice. Okay, Nisha, can you turn your pain into empowerment? Can you turn your grief into action or service? Can this experience be transformative in your life? Yes, sometimes. But only sometimes. Perhaps we need to understand and accept that "sometimes" is enough.

• • •

WHAT IF MY MARRIAGE DOESN'T SURVIVE?

> All I know is since his death, as far as I'm concerned,
> our relationship absolutely went to hell. It's been like
> a nightmare. I didn't feel permission to grieve or to
> express my feelings very much. Bill didn't want
> to talk about it and I did.
>
> —Norma, age forty-nine, whose seventeen-year-old son had
> died in a sporting accident five years and two months earlier

Not all families remain intact after a severe emotional trauma. If there were cracks in the marriage before the death of your child, the added stress can be more than a marriage can bear. The problems you once experienced may be intensified and inflated because of the strain. My marriage ended just three years after Victor's death. It all seemed to dissolve so rapidly. My two children, Andrew and Fay, and I are extremely close, but it went so quickly from the five of us to the three of us. It was a painful time of a double dose of grief that sometimes melted into one dark cloud.

The statistics on divorce after the death of a child are unclear. Some parents report that the death of their child made their relationship stronger, while others say that their marriage fell apart after their child died. Family and friends, as well as bereaved couples, often mention they have heard that the great majority of couples divorce after the child's death. What's the truth? Sandy Fox writes that the actual divorce rate is much lower than the common belief. "The survey found that only 16 percent of the parents divorce after the death of a child and only 4 percent said it was because of the death. . . . [In many cases] there were problems in the marriage way before the child died" (http://www.opentohope.com/author/sfox). Surveys by The Compassionate Friends in both 1999 and 2006 showed no significant difference between divorce rates of parents who experienced the loss of a child and those of other couples (http://www.compassionatefriends.org /media/Surveys). Shirley Murphy, a retired professor at the University of Washington, conducted a study that tracked 271 bereaved couples over twenty-five years. She found that the oft-repeated assertion that losing a child destroys a relationship is not true. In fact, only a small number broke up. In my own research—admittedly not a representative sample—I did not find higher rates of divorce among the parents I interviewed than would be found in the general population. The difficulties that couples talked about as a result of their loss and bereavement did not necessarily result in divorce. As the author Bruce Feiler said in an article in the *New York Times*, "Love is bringing imaginativeness to the unimaginable. It's not a choice you make once but over and over again."

As revealed in the book *Devastating Losses*, the factor that seems to be most central to marital stability or fragility is whether or not a spouse felt helped and supported by his or her partner or felt that the partner increased stress and difficulty. If you feel that your marriage is no longer providing the comfort, love, and support that you need, or if your marriage has already dissolved, of course you are now dealing with an additional layer of pain and loss. You may feel that the ground has crumbled beneath your feet and that, one after another, things you thought would be stable and lasting have shattered.

People often ask me, "Did the death of your child break up your marriage?" My answer is, "No, but the experience assisted us in facing and dealing with issues that we had been avoiding out of fear of hurting each other or our children." A child's death can press you to become more honest and more yourself. You think, why not? What do I have to lose? How many times can I die? Victor's death made me question and face my priorities. It helped me to eventually become more truthful and to reevaluate my choices. It helped me to face myself and my marriage and make some hard choices that earlier I was too frightened to make. In some weird way, it forced me to become even more myself. This has not been pain-free, but it has been essential to my life's journey.

If you find yourself facing a separation or divorce, try to think of something each morning, even if it is only one small thing, that is positive about moving forward in a new way. You may feel inundated with loss, but I promise you there is a kernel of something positive in the changes you are experiencing. There were times when the loss of Victor, my marriage, and our family of five as I knew it was so excruciating I did not believe I could survive. How does one live with a broken heart? This to me is still the mystery and miracle. Now, many years later, I know that even as my grief was overwhelming, my healing was beginning. Please believe that yours is too.

• • •

Where am I finding strength?

The memories I had of Mark in our family are very vivid to me and a source of strength. All these memories that could not be taken away from me, they're mine. Mark is still one of us, part of our family circle. We always held hands and bowed heads at dinner. Now, when we do this, I visualize the circle and Mark is always part of the circle.

—Gail, age forty-six, whose seventeen-year-old son had died by suicide four years and eleven months earlier

Someone might already have suggested to you that the death of your child will make you stronger. Friends or associates may have said that this tragedy might make you and your family more appreciative of life or more compassionate. Statements like these can easily make you feel angry or resentful, or that the other person doesn't "get it." Yet there is a certain truth in what they're saying.

It is true that parents who have survived a year of grief and tragedy sometimes feel empowered by their survival. That is, they have a stronger sense of their own ability to confront the worst life has to offer and to push forward against those terrible headwinds. Camilla, who had lost her nine-day-old daughter to a congenital heart defect, said, "It felt good to have the first year over. It was as if the first anniversary was a milestone. I could look back and take a breath and say, 'I did it. I got through the worst of it a healthy human being.'"

Obviously, not everyone feels that way, and as we've said before, healing does not follow a strict timetable. The death of your child is still foremost in your mind and heart, but gradually you will probably become aware that you are finding new or renewed sources of strength, whether through your spiritual beliefs, your cherished memories, your connections with friends and family, your exercise or therapy, or the simple fact that you are surviving the worst life has to offer. Through the many years that I've had the privilege to talk with surviving family members, I've heard them mention these sources of strength and many others. But two things came up most consistently. One was helping others. So many parents spoke of the need to be available to help other grieving parents, and how deeply comforting this simple act was for them as well as the other parents.

The other insight I heard many times was that parents coped and found strength by incorporating into their own lives the qualities in their child that were so precious to them. Ace, whose daughter Lili was born with Apert syndrome and died unexpectedly in her sleep at age fifteen, said this: "The biggest impact it's had on my life is just to always imagine her courage and her smile and, you know, walk through the world with as much of that as I can."

That struck a chord for me. I told Ace I have always believed that when we miss someone, if we can integrate their characteristics that we admired and loved into our own lives, if we become more like them in those special ways, we keep them alive within ourselves. Brenda expresses a similar awareness: "She stays very present in my mind always. She was a caring child. She took flowers to people, she loved people, and she hugged them. These are things I can do in her place. That's one way she continues."

When I miss Victor terribly, I actively try to think of what I'm missing about him and then try to integrate that quality into my own life, try to become more like Victor in that way. If I miss his warmth and hugs—his hugs were the best!—I try to give that warmth to others, to become the warm, hugging person that he was. I don't miss those parts of him as much because they've become part of me and I can offer them to others.

• • •

How can I continue to help my children cope?

I would say our family is far closer than we ever were before. We express our feelings so much more than we ever did before, and we are more open with each other.

—Lu, age forty-one, whose seventeen-year-old son had died in an automobile accident six years earlier

Just as you have moved through the months of grief in this last year, so have your children. My daughter Fay described her experience in the first year after Victor died this way: "The extra space in the back seat of the car while driving. Family vacation to Kona without him. Empty chair at the table during dinner. Moving into his bedroom. Emptiness." The physical reminders of Victor's absence reflected for her a deep emotional emptiness and pain.

Even after a year has passed, it is typical for family members to try to protect each other by holding back feelings out of fear of upsetting someone. Sometimes family members simply aren't ready to openly express their difficult feelings and pain. Myrna's fourteen-year-old daughter had died in a riding accident eleven months earlier. Myrna realized her son Jack, now sixteen, who had been very close to his sister, needed to process his loss according to his own timetable.

I asked Myrna how she helped her son, especially since he was being a typical teen, into his friends, his music. "We tried to just kind of be where he was at and, you know, let him know that we were there for him, and pick him up and take him places, fix his breakfast each morning, make sure he had what he needed. That's what we did. And [we] just kept letting him know how much we love him. But it was still very hard for him to see us sad.

"He would tell me that 'you're here for me, you're doing things for me, but you're not really here for me.' I wasn't the happy person I was before, and so in his mind I wasn't there for him emotionally. I was there for him physically, and he let me know that. And then sometimes, like when we talked about it, then I would buy a card and write something in it, or try and get him to spend some time with me, and just ask a lot about his life."

Another mother, Bonnie, told me of the bond between her sixteen-year-old daughter and eighteen-year-old son. After her son died in a car accident, she said, "I forced my-self to get up and get out of bed every day. Sad as I was, I tried to not check out on [my daughter]. The other thing I did, I remember people offering to give her a ride to cello lessons or whatever. And I'm like, 'No. I'm still her mom. I can do it.' I knew that she had lost her best friend and I didn't want her to think she lost her parents, too."

Without question, to be present emotionally for your other children when you are hurting and distraught is one of the biggest challenges. Though my son Andrew and daughter Fay have grown into loving, compassionate adults, I still wish I had been more present for them after Victor's death, less caught in the whirlpool of my own emotions. It is not uncommon for parents, looking back, to have these thoughts. But it is always possible to make a renewed com-mitment to spend time with your children, to do some-thing special to express your love, and to talk with them.

● ● ●

How do we keep our child
as a part of our family?

I knew for sure since I was thirteen years old that I would
name a child after Victor. Isn't that part of the healing? I
mean, in terms of how do we integrate our loved ones when
they pass? And it's like, well, we incarnate this beautiful
spirit of them and what we loved about them and we imbue
those qualities in our new loved ones. So I love that.

—Fay, my daughter, age fifty, whose older brother Victor had
died in a hiking accident in Yosemite in 1980 when she was
thirteen

It is Jewish tradition to name a new child after a relative
who has passed away and whose beloved qualities you
want to see continued in a future generation. My daughter, Fay, is named after my grandmother. Fay named one of
her daughters Miriam, after my mother, and one daughter
Victoria, after Victor. As mentioned before, my son Andrew and his wife Sarah named their two daughters Violet and Ruby Valentina—yup, names that begin with "V."
My brother Elliott, who married and had children late in
life, named his son Victor, and all of these kids know exactly who they're named after. Fay says, "My friends know
about Victor. My kids know about Victor. My ex-husband
knows about Victor. I don't think there's anybody who
knows me that doesn't know about Victor. And not just
that I had a brother who died, but about Victor, who he
was, and who he is to me."

My friend Kristin said her mother, Gerd Jakob, told
her a Norwegian proverb she heard from her grandfather
Tom in Norway: "I am not forgotten as long as my name

is still spoken." I think of this impulse, throughout different cultures and times, to keep our loved ones with us. It is part of healing, as my daughter Fay insightfully says. We speak their names and remember their precious spirits. You remember who they were and are to you, their essence that you value and love so deeply.

It used to be that people assumed the way to heal from loss was to "let go" of the loved one. We now know, and much research shows, that when we maintain connection through dreams, memories, visions, or rituals, we enrich our lives and promote well-being. I am thrilled that research now supports what bereaved parents and families have known all along. Instead of severing our bond, to mourn means to maintain a continuing relationship with our child and to integrate our loved one into our life in a new way.

Some families put together beautiful memory books, with contributions from their child's friends and other family. Several I've known have gathered family videos into a commemorative film. One mother assembled scrapbooks of her daughter's memorabilia, and another sewed a special quilt from her child's favorite clothing. Pamela AP told me of something she did that made me smile.

After the death of Pamela's daughter, Gabri, a friend sent her a box of heart-shaped rocks. At first she was hurt even more because all she had was a box of rocks instead of her daughter. Then she began noticing heart-shaped rocks when she took a hike, and began collecting them. She and her friend began exchanging photos of the hearts they would find—leaves like a heart, a heart in the cappuccino—"and before you know it, I've spent the last

two-and-a-half years surrounded by hearts, and love it."
Eventually, she decided to embed these special heart-
shaped rocks in cement as one of the steps up to a meditation platform that her husband built. In this way, her
daughter's loving presence greets her each time she goes to
meditate.

All of these ideas, and many others, are excellent ways
to give your child a special presence in your life that en-
capsulates her unforgettable spirit. They are loving, healing gestures that help others know what your child means
to you, to your family, and to so many others.

Continue to talk about your child, to tell stories about
him, to include him in your conversations. If it feels right
for you, use social media such as Facebook pages and
online memorial sites. Keep her picture on display with
your other family photos, or display his favorite football
jersey. Encourage your children and partner to talk about
her and to know that she will always be a precious part of
your family. Lu, whose seventeen-year-old son had died
in an automobile accident six years earlier, says, "Everything pleasurable that happens in our family, anything bad
that happens in our family, you want to share it. You still
think, 'I have to tell Derek.' Or you want to include him
in it. That never stops. I hope it never does."

• • •

How can I protect my health
as grief takes its toll?

I'm out of breath a lot. I don't have the physical stamina
I used to. I don't like the fact that I've allowed myself to
become physically unhealthy, but I'm not doing anything
about it. So am I punishing myself? In a way, I think it all
stems back to: nothing matters. Nothing matters.

—Lolly, age forty, whose eighteen-year-old daughter had
died in an automobile accident one year earlier

Research shows that grief affects people physically, and I
was told over and over after Victor died to take care of
myself physically because I was "at risk." Yet I wasn't
sure what that meant. Would physical activity help? Even
though I had been a marathon runner and dancer for years,
physical exercise initially felt impossible. My body felt like
a block of wood. Maybe taking care of myself meant I
should rest more, or that I needed more sleep, or to eat
more healthfully. I wasn't sure. But I did manage to slowly
get back to some running and swimming. And I tried to
get as much sleep as I could.

Suddenly, five years after Victor's death, I ruptured
a thoracic disc in my back directly behind my heart and
lungs. I saw several doctors who were all surprised at the
location of the rupture. "Highly unusual," they repeated
over and over. That particular area of the spine doesn't
usually rupture unless there is a severe impact such as an
automobile accident or fall. I had had none. But couldn't a
severe emotional impact do the same? My physicians were
sure there was no connection between this rupture and my
grief, but I remember a bomb exploding in my chest when

I got the news of Victor's death. The acupuncturist called the ruptured disc "a broken heart." Was it the case that my broken heart just couldn't take it anymore? I was in a full-body steel back brace for two years.

In fact, research shows that shock, pain, and grief consume a lot of energy. Stress uses body protein in the same way that vigorous activity does. No wonder you feel exhausted! And that means you have to spend extra time rebuilding and replenishing your body, mind, and spirit. If you're unable to nurture and nourish your body in healthful ways, you may find that the stress will cause some weak point in your body to give way. You start catching more colds than usual, or a simple cold turns to pneumonia. Your back gives out; your arthritic knees get worse.

Please take care of yourself during this crisis time and throughout the years to come. Take your exhaustion to heart and allow yourself to do the things you know will help reduce your stress and revitalize you. Give yourself permission to sleep more and to engage in restful activities. If you are a meditator, meditate. If you are new to meditating, learn more about meditating and try it. Eat a healthful diet. Consider joining an exercise group, a sports team, or a dance class. Be open to trying things that you haven't done before. Often exercise is easier and more fun when you have a regularly scheduled time with others. And good exercise will release those mood-enhancing endorphins, your body's natural way of feeling better.

Engage in mindful walking—more like a stroll looking at nature around you. Walk, walk, walk and bring your attention to your breath. No need to change your breathing—just noticing it helps calm you. Breathing deeply is difficult when we are trying not to feel. Taking a shallow breath or deeply sighing are natural physical experiences while grieving. With time you will be able to breathe more regularly and easily again. When you nourish yourself, you help your body as well as your mind to heal.

If you find that these steps toward self-care remain difficult, I encourage you to tell yourself that you are worth it. Pamela Ashkenazy, a grief counselor and therapist whose only son Daniel died, writes: "One of the challenges for self-care for [mothers] was that they needed to first make the decision that their lives were worth living despite their sorrow and grief." If you find that the healthy activities that you know would help are too hard to do, that you can't find the motivation or don't feel that it matters, please talk to a grief counselor who can help you work through the obstacles, or find a grief support group. That alone will be a way of taking care of you.

• • •

WHAT IF I FIND MYSELF WORKING, EATING, OR DRINKING TOO MUCH?

I stopped exercising. I stopped watching what I eat; I gained weight. I can almost feel like I'm so fragile that I can't do anything. All I can do is just the simplest of things.

—Pamela AP, age fifty-eight, whose seventeen-year-old daughter had jumped from the Golden Gate Bridge two years and six months earlier

When we are in deep grief, we often self-medicate. Some people start eating too much or turning to sugar. Some people start spending too much or drinking too much. We self-medicate because the pain is so deep and hard to handle. When Victor died, I started eating sugar and flour and stuffing my face to try to anesthetize myself. My addiction was sugar and flour and food. But it's not uncommon to try to anesthetize yourself with alcohol, over-immersion in work, or other unhealthy but distracting behaviors. One mother shared with me that her husband was dealing with his grief by overspending on his hobby of collecting coins.

Not long ago, my daughter Fay confided that she, too, turned to food as a salve for her wounds. She said that in the days immediately after Victor's death, "I remember going into the kitchen and sitting at the table and people would bring food and somebody said to me, 'Eat.' And they put this crumb cake in front of me. And I ate the entire cake. I remember eating the entire cake and not feeling anything inside. But I knew that that was some kind of a solution. That very first time, it was that, ah, I don't like how I'm feeling. What can I do to change my feeling?" Food, as well as alcohol, is definitely one of the drugs we use to numb ourselves, and obesity is common in the bereaved community.

To avoid falling into these easy but destructive habits, we have to learn to be comfortable with being uncomfortable, when we are alone and when we are with others. There are going to be many uncomfortable moments, such as when you hear other people talk about their children or you listen to insensitive comments. When you have to deal with anniversaries and birthdays or simply have to get through those dark, grief-stricken nights. You know what your triggers are, I'm sure. How do we deal with our sadness, pain, grief, resentment, anger? Do we eat? Drink? Overspend? Or do we learn new tools, better ways to help us navigate the shoals of grief?

One such tool is to recognize the red flags. Are you easily fatigued? Not engaging as often in your usual activities? Have you stopped exercising? Are you eating more sugar and carbs than you used to? Are you turning too often to alcohol or drugs? If you can answer "yes" to any of these questions, I urge you to reach out to a good friend, a support group, or a qualified professional who can help you through this difficult time. You do not have to make needed changes on your own. You only need to recognize the red flags and take the step of reaching out to someone to talk about your concerns.

• • •

WHAT DO I DO WHEN FRIENDS DON'T UNDERSTAND MY FEELINGS OR NEEDS?

Most people wanted to just avoid the subject of Steve. He's gone, that's it. We don't want to bring up any painful memories. But I think my experience was that once he was dead, people didn't want to talk about him. There were some times when I wanted to talk about him, and people would say, "Oh yes, but . . ." and go on to something else.

—Sonya, age forty-one, whose sixteen-year-old son had died in a fall three years and two months earlier

Feeling betrayed by those friends who don't provide the support you expected is a common sentiment among bereaved parents. Sonya put it bluntly: "I came right out with it. I said, 'I didn't think that when Steve died we'd be losing you, too.'" The feeling of a double loss when friends are unsupportive, of loss upon loss, is a difficult one to bear. It's natural to feel angry and let down.

Gail said, "One of the most difficult things for me was to accept that people, after a very short period of time, acted like he never lived. I say, 'Hey, I have to talk about him. He's real. He was.' And they don't want to talk about it. And I think that's another reason why this year in particular has been very difficult for me."

The sad fact is that our society, in general, doesn't deal well with death and bereavement. If you have friends who react with fear and avoidance or who offer platitudes and change the subject, they are simply reflecting this reality. One mother told me, "People that you thought were friends turn around and walk the other way. 'Hey, you touched death. I don't want you near me. Maybe it'll happen to me, to one of mine.'" It's almost as if you carry a contagion and others back away out of self-protection. Death, especially the death of a child, can carry stigma and evoke anxiety in others. Avoidance and distancing are, unfortunately, an all-too-common response. The death of a child is not a contagious disease!

If you feel disappointed in this way, please remind yourself that you are not alone. Many friendships flounder in the face of intense grief. What you do in response is up to you. You may choose to accept the gift of friendship even if it is not everything you want. Usually, some steadfast friends remain by your side, and you can talk openly about your child with them. They are the ones who are comfortable with your mention of your child's name and who kept faith that you would eventually move through the early periods of shattering grief. You may also have found a special kinship with other parents who had children who died, possibly because of their willingness to talk openly about their children. These new friendships may be where you now find understanding and support.

• • •

WHAT IF MY RELATIONSHIP TO MY CHILD STILL FEELS UNFINISHED?

> Like when I put on that coat Wednesday, I remembered when we went to buy her a coat and the conversation we had. And I just started thinking about how much I miss her. And I'd like to touch and hold her. And I envisioned telling her how much I missed her.
>
> —Kit, age fifty-six, whose seventeen-year-old daughter had died in an auto accident three years and eight months earlier

During this first year, you may have been flooded by memories of your child, some bringing solace and some deeply painful. If those memories are tinged with all the things you wish you'd said or that problem the two of you never quite resolved, they can evoke regret and anguish. There is so much pain connected to unfinished relationships. According to psychologist and process worker Dr. Arnold Mindell, "A lot of sadness about death is due to our own unfinished relationship with the deceased. Most of the time, we have become stuck in our relationship to them and do not find it possible to get to the eternal side of the relationship. We cannot let them go, we remain upset and sad or angry because we have not found our way to that precious something we are looking for."

If you feel that some unfinished business holds you back, you might try writing a letter to your child, telling him all that is in your heart. Write the words that you have been speaking in your head. Include everything that has come up for you, even that thought or feeling that you hesitate to mention or that you'd rather ignore. When you're done, put the letter in a special place. Add more letters as the days, weeks, and months pass, whenever you feel something welling up inside you that you want to say to her. If you find it easier, speak aloud to your child and tell her what is in your heart at this moment. Do whatever you need to do to complete the communication, to speak the unspoken. Do what you must to finish the unfinished. It is never too late to say what you need to say.

One father told his son in a letter all the things he had not had a chance to say before his sudden death. This allowed the father not only to vent his emotions but also to relieve his feeling of being cut off so abruptly from his child. Another mother I spoke with described how she would wake up late at night, full of tears and pain. Not wanting to awaken her husband or children, she would go into the family room and talk into a tape recorder. It was her way of working through worries and questions, and she often directed her conversation to her child, telling him how she missed him. In addition to speaking or writing to your child, you can also write yourself a letter *from* your child. It is a lovely thing to do.

When you write or talk about your feelings, you have a better chance of understanding yourself as well as your relationship with your child. Let your heart speak and trust that this speaking will be heard in the way it needs to be.

• • •

How can I feel a psychic or spiritual connection with my child?

> I hadn't any experiences of intuition until after Larry's death. But from then on, it was like I was in touch with something that I was not in touch with [before]. Something that I did not comprehend. Well, more and more I kept having little things happen and great things happen. And now, there's just a feeling of presence. Every time I'd be kind of feeling alone, somehow or other there would come to me some little sign.
>
> —Myra, age forty-seven, whose seventeen-year-old son had died in a pool accident four years and three months earlier

A psychic or spiritual connection with your child is available to you if you are open to it. It is that simple. Many parents experience such a connection, even those who have not thought of themselves as particularly spiritual before. Parents talk of these experiences as an intuitive sense of their child's presence, or as a feeling that their dead child is nearby and in communion with them. Sometimes the contact takes the form of a dream or sometimes a synchronicity, a coincidence that feels too remarkable and meaningful to be an accident. I have had many of these blessed moments myself. The year after Victor's death, my mother and I went to a restaurant for a Mother's Day brunch together. My mother was a great model to me of determination and love of life. She and Victor adored each other. On the last Mother's Day that Victor was alive, we went to her home and he cooked omelets for us. He had just learned how. He was so proud.

On this first Mother's Day without Victor, we were talking about my children, her grandchildren, and wondered if Victor would let us hear from him. It is a good thing my mother was there to witness what I saw next or I would have thought I was going bonkers. When we walked out of the restaurant, right in front of us two cars parked side by side displayed license plates that read "LUV" and "VIC." We just looked at each other and smiled. Of course!

A therapy client of mine whose daughter died of a sudden illness said to me, "If I could just have a sense of her presence, that would help. But I'm not a believer in dreams or such things." I told her my LUV VIC story. She smiled and admitted that a friend of hers had had a vivid dream in which her daughter appeared in a white, flowing gown, in the form of an angel, and had spoken to her of love. My client started to cry as she told this story and admitted that that was exactly how she thought of her daughter, as an angel in white, flowing robes. The image she carried of her daughter matched her friend's dream exactly. "I don't know," she said, "but I sure hope the dream is true!" For the first time, I saw a twinkle in her moist blue eyes.

If you have experienced these kinds of synchronicities or feelings of connection with your child, you know how they can light up your heart. They are truly blessings, moments when we feel the vastness and mystery of a world larger than our own. Mitch Carmody, whose young son died of a brain tumor, calls these signs "whispers of love." They are moments when we are touched by the loving grace of the universe.

If you haven't experienced a connection with your child but want to, there are many ways to pay attention. Notice synchronicities, slips of the tongue, feelings of intuition, or signs such as the unexpected appearance of two white butterflies or an animal like a deer. Marti, whose son was murdered seventeen years earlier, says,

> I look for him all the time, not in this physical realm that we live in, but I look for him in the spiritual realm and he shows up all the time. Guy [my husband] and I were driving down the highway, and there were a bunch of beautiful clouds. I said, 'Lance, are you there? If you are, show me a heart.' Five minutes later, Guy goes, 'Good God,' and he stops the car and looks up. And there's a perfect heart in the sky. So all of those things indicate to me that there's a spiritual realm that we connect to with our loved ones. I don't think that when you're in deep grief you're open to it. I think that you have to have the faith that they're there and they're going to help you. They're going to be part of your life.

· · ·

How can my dreams help me?

I had a dream of my son in which he said, "Hi, Mom."
And I said, "Hi, Son, I'm glad to see you. How come
you're here? Are you alright?" And he said, "I really
am alright, Mom. I just want you to know it's not
so bad here with Jesus."

—Joan, age forty-nine, whose twenty-one-year-old son
had died in a sporting accident three years and four
months earlier

You may see your child alive in dreams so vivid that it is a
shock all over again to wake up and remember your child
is dead. These can be painful moments that combine feelings of closeness and distance in a wrenching way. Pamela
AP, whose daughter Gabri unexpectedly jumped from the
Golden Gate Bridge at age seventeen, told me, tearfully,
of recurring dreams in which she was trying to save her
daughter. She was understandably distraught. We talked
more, especially about the fact that Pamela felt a strong
need for some proof of her daughter's spirit. I asked her if
she had felt her daughter's spirit and her face softened.

"I should be thankful for that first night when she
came to me, and we were merging like two energy balls.
It's like we had our arms wrapped around each other, but
we didn't really have arms. And she withdrew her face and
she was just beaming, smiling, so ecstatically happy. And
she told me, 'You don't have to let go until you're ready.' It
happened at four o'clock in the morning."

"Wow, so she came to you."

"I believe so."

"And she looked happy."

"She was ecstatic."

"That's her gift to you," I said. "That's a very important message. When you said, 'I don't want to think of her being nothing, not existing,' I thought, 'you bet.' I feel the same way. I understand. But when I allow myself to remember Victor's smile and twinkle and his joy, that spirit somehow soothes my aching heart."

"I sort of believe," Pamela went on, "that she knew she had to do something for me to survive. So that's the gift she gave me. That's usually how I choose to think about it."

I encouraged Pamela to continue thinking that way and to call up Gabri's powerful, ecstatic spirit whenever Pamela felt the need to be close to her and to feel her nearby. I vividly remember many dreams of Victor. He appears to reassure me, "Mom, all is well. I am here. I love you. Love is all there is."

The language of dreams is one of image and emotion, as is the language of spirit. Dreams can be a translator between worlds. Not everyone has the kind of experience Pamela describes, but if you're open, your dreams can be a channel for communication with and from your child. Keep a pen and paper by your bedside and take a moment upon waking to write down any dream or fragment you remember, even if fleeting. The more you pay attention, the more likely it is that your dreams will appear. You might select a lovely journal or blank book to write in, or decorate one yourself, making a collage on or painting the cover. When you have a special place to hold your inner visions, you're inviting them in.

●　●　●

How is my relationship to my God changing?

I definitely believe in God. There has to be a God; there has to be. I want him to take care of Bill, even though he didn't on that morning on the river.

—Sharon, age fifty, whose twenty-one-year-old son had died in a boating accident nine months earlier

In my research and my work with bereaved parents, I have found a wide range in the way that grief affects a parent's belief in God. Most parents affirmed and renewed their faith in God after their child's death as their connection to the spiritual world was strengthened. Their ongoing awareness of spirit supported their beliefs, and their beliefs in turn helped them through their crisis. One father whose four-year-old son drowned says that talking with other people didn't help his loss or pain. The only thing he was able to do was to stay close to God. His faith is what gave him strength.

Other parents I spoke with after a year or more had passed were still angry, and some disavowed God's existence even more strongly than immediately after their child's death. These parents chose to turn away from religious practices or beliefs, such as having faith in a benevolent God who personally conducts all aspects of our lives. They continued to find that image of God impossible to reconcile with what had happened to their child. Says Sonya, "I think that Steve's death has intensified my nonbelief. How could God do that? I don't believe in God as an all-powerful being anymore."

I remember talking with Jacob, whose twenty-three-year-old son had died three years earlier in a hit-and-run accident, and being touched by how he turned around this despair. "If it were true we could be protected, that God could save people, we would not be human. We would be robots. We wouldn't be human. We have horror and death and tragedy as part of the proof of the Great Spirit." He found tragedy to be evidence of a spiritual presence large enough to embody both good and evil. To him a God that offered only "good" things could not contain the fullness and mystery of life. This thinking is in line with that of the Jewish mystics, who say God is present but hidden. This leaves it up to us to find the hidden grace.

If you're interested in keeping up a conversation within yourself about your beliefs, it can be useful to write down what's in your heart from time to time and to see, over time, how your feelings change. Note your thoughts, desires, convictions, intensity of feeling, questions. Even for nonbelievers, this kind of reflection can prove valuable, as our feelings are rarely without nuance or unchanging.

• • •

How do I find a new sense of meaning and purpose in life?

I wouldn't want to lay a trip on [other grieving parents by] saying, "Well, if you really want to get over your grief, what you have to do is find something meaningful to come out of this." But I think, I do think that's mainly what happens.

—Cheryl, age forty-seven, whose eight-year-old son and twelve-year-old daughter had died in a plane crash eight years earlier

I have heard from so many bereaved parents that helping others, being compassionate toward others in their grief, has been a strong motivating force as they journey through life after loss. Bernie, whose five-and-a-half-year-old daughter Lynnel had died in a car accident fifty years earlier, tells the story of watching a TV program about two young lovers whose parents didn't approve of their relationship and who then died by suicide. "And the rest of the story is about the four parents and how one buried himself in work and one hit the bottle and this sort of thing. And I saw myself right then. I said, 'Bernie, you have a choice of what you are going to do with all this grief.' And I [noticed] the one woman, the one mother in this foursome, said, 'The only way I'm going to get through it myself is to be present with other grieving people, to learn and then to give.' I went, 'Yeah,' and that's what I've done."

Finding new purpose is an area in which you have a choice, in which you can feel empowered. You can decide how you want to move ahead. Right now, you may not feel ready to do anything more than get through each day. That is a lot! But when the time is right, you can think about how you can bring meaning and purpose more strongly into your life.

Ayesha, whose daughter had died in a fire eight years earlier, says,

> It changes people, just as an amputation, the loss of a limb would. I think you see it either as the end of your world or you see it as a new challenge to learn how to live life without one life, or without one arm. A loss of a child is a handicap for the rest of your life. I sought out people to help me and people for me to help. And that's how I've gotten through it. I think I've gotten through it as a stepping stone rather than a stumbling block to my growth. She has made me more than I would have been. Her life was not a waste. Even though she had enormous potential and it was cut short. It wasn't wasted.

One of the most painful aspects of losing a child is that his or her life was so brief. His short life and sudden death have affected relatively few people on this planet. You saw so much vitality, creativity, and potential that will not be realized. That can seem sad, even tragic. Then again, maybe that's limited thinking. Maybe a child has more impact than some people who live their full life span and die in their nineties. Maybe our children can teach us to make our lives count.

PART 4

As the Years Go By,
What Can I Expect?

My Story: Windy Hill

March 1, 1993, Windy Hill, Portola Valley, California

Almost thirteen years after Victor's death, I hike up to Windy Hill, part of a nature preserve south of San Francisco, passing through stands of bay and oak, inhaling the musky scent of bay leaves and earth. The wind always blows here, stirring the rich mix of vegetative smells. At the top I sit on the bench overlooking Portola Valley. Sometimes I drive up the curving road of Skyline Boulevard and then walk the ten minutes to the bench. But today I hike for an hour and a half up the hill, through grasslands and redwoods, shade and sun. When I reach the top, I'm relieved to be welcomed by the now familiar tranquility and beauty of Victor's wooden bench. The bronze plaque on the back of the bench reads: "In loving remembrance of Victor Robinson Zenoff, July 19, 1962–July 12, 1980, who loved the beauty and freedom of these hills." I notice some kids have carved their initials and a heart into the wood on the side of the bench. Victor would have liked that.

I sit quietly on the bench. What a beautiful spot this is, with its sweeping view of grassy hilltops, sky and clouds, a white-tailed kite gliding in broad, smooth circles above, the humming valley spread below. Elon proposed to Fay here two years ago with three red roses in hand. I leave for their wedding two weeks from today—I'm so excited.

I think there will be a full moon tonight. I sit in the wind, listening to the faint traffic noise from the valley, when suddenly a thought disrupts my meditation. That man who called me last fall. Who was he? Where did he come from? Did I ever thank him for calling? I am so grateful for the story he told me.

I was staying with friends in Portland, Oregon, last October, attending a class on Process Work, a cross-disciplinary approach to facilitating individual and collective change conducted by a teacher and colleague of mine, Dr. Arny Mindell. Friday evening I called into my answering machine in Palo Alto and heard a message from a stranger. His deep voice said, "Please give me a call. It's about your son Victor."

I thought I must have heard the message incorrectly. I dialed my Palo Alto number again. The same message repeated. My body began to shake. I knew Victor was dead. That was the reality. Yet for a moment my imagination took over and I had the ultimate forbidden thought. Maybe Victor is really alive after all! No, no, that's impossible. I saw the photograph of Victor's body in that horrible blue body bag up in Yosemite. I know that was my son.

I didn't mention anything to my friends Kate and Joe. I slept restlessly. The next morning, when the house was empty and quiet, I dialed the number in California.

"This is Nisha Zenoff. Are you the person that called about my son, Victor?" I was nervous, trembling.

"Yes." The man's voice sounded the same as on my machine.

"Well, what do you want?" I asked impatiently.

"You're the Zenoff whose son, Victor, died, and you put a bench up on Windy Hill in his memory, right?"

"Yes."

"Well, one day a few weeks ago, when I was close to the end of my line, I went hiking up to Windy Hill. I had recently gone through a difficult divorce, and life didn't seem much worth living anymore. So I went to Windy Hill to decide how I was going to end my life."

I grabbed my yellow pad to take notes and began scribbling.

"I always walk right past that bench. But this time as I walked past it, I suddenly heard a voice. No, it was more like I felt a strong force coming from that bench into my back. I couldn't walk away. It pulled me back. It wouldn't take no for an answer.

"Then out of that strong force came the most amazing, incredible, all-loving presence. I know it was your son, Victor. He was a huge presence, larger than anything I had ever experienced. All light and all love. He spoke to me and said, 'It is all about love. You never have to worry. Love is all there is.'

"Then he told me to find his mother, to find you and tell you that he knows you love him and that you are love. That he loves you and that you are never alone. Never. There is nothing, absolutely nothing, to ever fear. It is all okay, and it is all about the everlasting all-presence of love, the all-presence of love that can never be destroyed.

"Then the force vanished as quickly as it appeared. But something changed in me in that moment. I continued walking past the bench, this time all the way to the end of the path. I knew I would live my life. That bench. Your son. That presence gave me my life back, and I want to thank you."

Then he was quiet. I was in shock and wondered what I had just heard. I quietly thanked him for calling.

Before we said good-bye, he asked if we could meet sometime in Palo Alto. I told him about a lecture that I would be attending in three weeks and that perhaps we could say hello there. I put down the phone and sat alone, hearing his words over and over in my mind, not quite sure what had just happened or with whom I had just talked. I couldn't mention the phone call to anyone for days, until finally I spoke with Arny about it.

"Your son is talking to you," he said. "Listen to what he is saying." I have been listening ever since.

Several weeks later, at the Zen Center in San Francisco, I attended a lecture on working with the dying. During the break, I heard a voice asking, "Are you Victor's mom?"

I was shocked. It had been years since anyone referred to me that way. I loved it. My heart jumped and danced. I was thrilled.

"Yes, I sure am!" I jumped up out of my chair. There in front of me stood the man who had called. We shook hands and smiled knowingly at each other. The lecture began again, and he vanished in the crowd. I never saw him again.

I sit quietly on the bench, looking out over the valley. These days when I think of Victor, it usually doesn't cause me pain. Rather, my heart is filled with joy and warmth for his very being. I see his smiling face, his dimple, his long, wavy brown hair and brown leather handmade boots. He was and is a part of my life and always will be. He is no longer just my son. He has become one of my important teachers, as are my other two children. My heart feels full and at peace. The wind brushes against my cheeks and blows my hair into my eyes. I am invigorated by it. I breathe it in.

I take another deep breath. The breeze feels soothing against my skin. And now the wind is still, at least for a moment. I feel humbled by the beauty and the mystery of it all.

• • •

WHEN DOES THE PAIN BECOME BEARABLE?

People can look at me and say, "Oh, you made it." And I can honestly say, "Yes, I made it." Not, "Well, I may make it and I may not." It wasn't that all of a sudden I felt okay about their being dead. I didn't, of course. But there was a quality of my grief that changed. It was still painful, but there wasn't that wrenching part to it. It was gone.

—Cheryl, age forty-seven, whose eight-year-old son and twelve-year-old daughter had died in a plane crash eight years earlier

Not long ago I attended a meeting of The Compassionate Friends for the first time in many years. I accompanied a newly bereaved parent who didn't want to go by herself. The meeting was loving, comforting, and gentle.

My friend was glad she went and will go back to the next meeting. The leaders, all parents who have experienced the death of a child, were kind, nonjudgmental, open, and warm. I realized I was the "elder" there, the parent with the most years—thirty-seven—since the death of my child. The others were hungry to ask me, "What is it like down the road?" "Do you still think of Victor the first thing each morning when you wake up?" "Do you remember when your pain changed and became bearable?"

The Compassionate Friends meeting was a safe and sacred place for sharing not only grief but, surprisingly, humor and abundant love. I was grateful that I could be supportive of others and so grateful to realize how far my journey has taken me.

It's hard to say exactly when the time came that the most searing, unbearable pain began to shift for me. Many years down the road I could still be doubled over with pain and grief. Yet I also, gradually, began to feel propelled back to a new, purposeful life.

Bonnie, whose eighteen-year-old son had died in a car accident nine years earlier, described her grief process this way:

> I cried 24/7 for close to a year, I think. Then I cried every day at some point during the day for a very long time. For some people I think it's a few months and some people it's a couple years, but at some point, for me the big turning point in feeling better in general was when I started remembering him and how he lived and not how he died. For so long, every time I closed my eyes I thought about how he died. Not that I still don't think about him every second, but I don't think

about, 'Oh my God, he died,' and the whole accident thing happens. By the two-year mark it was still there, but it wasn't happening to me every night anymore. [When I could] think about Philip and not about Philip's accident . . . I think that makes the biggest difference in the world for all of us as grieving parents. [The shift happened] when I started thinking about him as a person as opposed to how his life ended.

Many parents report feeling worse at the three-month mark or the two-year mark, times when the numbness may start wearing off or the reality of what happened sinks in further. Ginny, whose fifteen-year-old son had died in a car accident twenty-seven years earlier, had attended Compassionate Friends meetings when her son died and had been forewarned that this could happen.

When I got to the three months and everybody [friends] went away and I was feeling worse, I didn't feel so bad because somebody had said that at three months it's the hardest and two years is the hardest. Everybody is different, but just so you don't wake up on the second year and think, "I have made so much progress, what the hell is the matter with me? I've never been so miserable." Then you go, "Oh, somebody told me. I don't have to worry. This is normal. This is natural."

And that whole thing that Kübler-Ross said about, you know, here are the stages of grief. After we had gone through it for the first three months, [my husband] Will said, "She was right about the stages, but," he said, "they happen every hour." Ginny laughs. It's not like, oh the first week and you're. . . . That's what

we used to think when we read that. It was like, it's all
organized. Well, it's not organized.

Elisabeth Kübler-Ross contributed greatly to our understanding of death and dying. However, the stages of
grief she described were based on her work with the ill
and dying, not with bereaved parents. In "On Grief and
Grieving," Kübler-Ross herself wrote that the stages
"were never meant to help tuck messy emotions into neat
packages." As so many parents will say, the road through
bereavement is not a process through neat stages. A young
mother whose teenage son died suddenly of a medical
problem said to me recently, through tears, "Those stages
of grief are so misleading. I thought I was crazy because
they all come within minutes of each other." She was relieved to learn that she was not crazy and that other parents knew what she was experiencing.

In the years ahead, you will come to understand
and appreciate your own healing rhythms, which will
be unique to you. You will have steps forward and steps
back, days when you begin to feel a part of the world once
again and days when you need to retreat. But you will feel,
slowly, the reality of the healing force within, as you continue to be sustained by your love for your child.

• • •

WHEN IS GRIEVING FINISHED?

I don't think I'll ever be through grieving, but the message
that used to be in my head that said, "I can't survive, I can't

go on, this is too hard for me to take"—that's gone, even though the loss is still there. Just the fact that I'm living a normal life and I'm basically a happy person and have loving friends and family and it didn't throw me off the deep end or over the edge. I did, in fact, survive.

—Margie, age forty-eight, whose fifteen-year-old daughter had died in an automobile accident eight years and ten months earlier

No one needs to describe grief to you: the loss of appetite, sleeping problems, heart palpitations, headaches, stomach pains, chest pains, thoughts of death and self-destruction. For many parents, the intensity of such effects lessens as they move into the ongoing time of living with the loss of their child. In this transition period, you are probably no longer suffering from the tornado, but there are still likely to be stormy times. Thankfully, there will also be times of greater ease, even of pleasure. You are gathering strength and knowledge from your experiences. You are becoming a person who has survived and grown from a terrible rite of passage.

As the years pass, you will begin to define and accept what you have experienced and to live with it, maybe even make sense of it in some way that feels right to you. However, as research suggests, grieving after a child's death is never actually finished, although the experience of mourning certainly changes over time. In his book, *Grief Counseling and Grief Therapy*, psychologist William Worden observes that "asking when mourning is finished is a little like asking how high is up." During the first few years, you probably remembered and missed your child with a pain as brutal as a physical attack. Now, as time passes, you can think of your child often and feel comforted and nurtured. Sadness does not disappear, but many parents are able to think of their children without excruciating pain. And eventually with joy, happiness, and gratitude.

On those days when sadness sweeps through you again, even if at a duller pitch, please remember the idea of "shadow grief" suggested by psychologists Ronald Knapp and Larry Peppers—the grief that persists in the background of our days and is recognized by grief researchers as part of the ongoing process of loss. Shadow grief is the intense sadness that overcomes us when least expected. Shakespeare recognized this centuries ago: "My grief lies all within. And these external manners of lament are mere shadows to the unseen grief that swells with silence in the tortured soul" (*Richard II*).

This understanding can bring relief of its own, as you can remind yourself that what you're feeling is part of the natural course of healing. If you still feel these fluctuations in your bereavement experience, know that your body and mind are healing in the way that they are meant to. Even though time has passed, you still have every right to express your grief. If you need to, put aside time each day, private moments when you can feel whatever is in your heart without worrying about how your feelings affect your work, family, or friends.

If you feel isolated or worried about your continuing grief, it is not too late—it is never too late—to reach out to Compassionate Friends or other similar grief support groups. Lu said, "[Participating in Compassionate Friends] was a very good way to find out that, in fact, I was not going crazy, that this is the way everybody reacts." Individual or family therapy with a therapist trained in grief work

can also offer many resources to help you onward on your
deep healing journey.

. . .

WHAT IF I FEEL GUILTY ABOUT
FEELING BETTER?

I don't have to have this sort of causal relationship with my
brother. It can be that we are connected, but you know, by
blood and by family and by love and spirit, but that my life
is my own. I don't need to live in reaction to his life and
his loss anymore. I can be okay with being happy. I don't
think that Danny would want me to be unhappy.

—Susan L., age forty-nine, whose sixteen-year-old brother
had died of medical mismanagement of a congenital
disorder thirty-six years earlier

Grief has defined you and your relationship to your child
for some time now, and as you feel grief begin to lose its
sharpness, even a little, you may worry that your child,
too, will slip away. Grief is a way to stay connected and
close to our child. In grief, you are emotionally and spiritually united with her. She is alive through your strong
emotions, and you carry her through your days in that
way. What happens when you start to have moments when
you aren't consumed with grief or thinking of your child?
Will your child become less vivid, like a fading dream, less
alive in spirit?

"There's a part of it that seems unreal, very unreal,"
says Cheryl. "And looking back and thinking there was

that whole part of my life and it's gone." Sometimes these increasing feelings of distance from the physical reality of your child brings a flood of new feelings, such as guilt, renewed pain, or unease. As one mother said in the first year of grieving, "I'm uncomfortable when I feel better. It feels wrong."

When parents express these concerns, I always tell them that their bond with their child is not fading or disappearing, only changing as it should. You are learning to tolerate and integrate into your life the finality of your child's death. It may seem strange that what once felt like a totally broken heart is capable of opening itself again, to the world, to others, to feelings of love and appreciation. But of course that is a positive shift. You will not be held in the most catastrophic grief through endless time.

Kelly Osmont, LCSW, a grief counselor whose nineteen-year-old son died after being kicked by a horse, writes in her book *More Than Surviving: Caring for Yourself While You Grieve* that we are not closer to our loved ones when we are in pain. "A belief which inhibits healing is thinking you are closer to your loved one when your heart aches than when you feel pleasure or peace. I used to think that when I felt sad I was closer to him. I learned that when I was at peace, or even laughing, I could also remember him with a deep love, as well."

One mother, Megan, told me how she understood the changes within her as she healed: "I would feel that I was really doing her a disservice if I wasn't a happy person. I would feel that she would be upset with me if I couldn't laugh and if I couldn't feel joy. Because she was a very, very happy, smiling type of person." Allowing feelings of pleasure and happiness to return to her life is, for Megan, a way of honoring her beloved child and expressing her child's spirit in the world. It is, paradoxically, a way to hold her close.

• • •

WILL I BEGIN TO FORGET MY CHILD?

She is still real in the presence of life. I don't see her or think of her with great sadness. So even though she is dead, the things she has been to my life, the delight, the joy, they don't stop in any way.

—Brenda, age forty-seven, whose five-year-old daughter had died in an automobile accident twenty years earlier

Once the shock and sorrow become less acute, many grieving parents begin to fear they will actually forget their child. Do not be anxious about this, for it simply does not happen. Your child is a part of your very cells, who you are on the most fundamental level, and that will not change. Your feelings for your child will always be with you, and the love you feel for your child will last forever. Just as the love remains, so does your relationship to your child. The form of the relationship will change, it is true. Because the physical relationship is gone, your child now lives in your heart, in your images and memories, in nature, dreams, visions, and fantasies.

It is this shift that can be disturbing, the loss of immediacy, of physicality. My daughter Fay expressed it this

way: "What scared me was . . . when the memories started
to slip because [initially] I could physically, like I could see
his skin, I could see his hair, I could smell him. I could
know the way he stands and what his clothes looked like.
And as the years went by, I couldn't quite remember his
voice or I couldn't quite remember things about him that
I, I just really needed."

What Fay said next touched my heart: "So once I
started letting go of his physical being I started to feel his
joy of life and his love. He had a huge heart. I felt like Victor's heart was so big it could flood the room. And his love
of nature. So I think that's one of the ways [I coped]."

Your child's brilliant, loving essence will never die.
It will always be with you. As you transition from being
used to the physical presence of your child to getting used
to the absence of the physical body, you forge a new and
powerful relationship, through dreams, visitations, memory, or spirit. As long as you are alive, so, too, is your relationship with your child alive. You can think of your
child's inimitable, powerful essence any time. You can renew and reaffirm your relationship whenever you feel the
need. When you fear that your child could fade from your
life, try spending some time with him.

Find a comfortable place where you can lie or sit com-
fortably, without interruption. Close your eyes and imagine yourself being with your child. Imagine both of you
alive, walking and playing together, or you may see both
of you together in spirit. The important thing is to feel
yourself together. Now tell your child anything that's in
your mind or your heart. Ask your child questions and listen to the answers. Feel the warmth and companionship as
you and your child share this moment. Or you might want

to simply say hello to your child each morning and good night each evening, thanking your child for her beautiful presence in the world and in your heart.

• • •

HOW CAN I KEEP MY CHILD WITH ME OVER TIME?

> I remember the wind blowing the scarf and the colors of the scarf and his happiness. And that gives me joy to remember that, waking up and remembering that and still being able to visualize him.
>
> —Patty, age fifty-five, whose seventeen-year-old son had died in an automobile accident fourteen years and seven months earlier

If there is one area in which your emotional needs might actually increase with time, it could be in your need for a greater connection with your child. The need to feel that your child is nearby and within your reach—whether through a spiritual, religious, or psychic experience or simply in your heart—tends to become stronger as the years pass. That initial powerful desire you had to be physically reunited with your child, expressed as the desire to join him or her in death, is perhaps lessened, but the need to remain connected persists.

Contrary to the view that over time we must slowly detach from our loved one in order to heal, many in the grief community now believe that finding ways to maintain enduring connections is an essential part of a healthy mourning process. Whether through internal dialogues

and dreams or through rituals and conversation, this ongoing bond is central to healing. In her Foreword to the
book *Passed and Present: Keeping Memories of Loved Ones
Alive*, author Hope Edelman refers to the work of psychologist Louise Kaplan when she writes, "To pretend those
relationships do not endure, or to deny ourselves the opportunity to maintain them, is to cast ourselves adrift, be-
reft, severed from relationships that might otherwise have
continued to sustain us."

The bereaved parents I have met over the years have
shared remarkable stories about how they remember their
child and reinforce their bond. Rituals can be especially
affirming, and many families develop deeply meaningful
rituals around their child's birthday and death day. Monica, whose almost-nineteen-year-old son was murdered six
years earlier, describes what her family does:

> Where he's buried is about an hour-and-a-half drive,
> and there's something about the drive and the time
> that it takes to get there, getting out of the city—we
> have, like, rituals. We always get the same food, and
> we bring chairs and gardening things, and we tend to
> his grave and scatter—I always collect flower petals—
> so every time we visit we usually scatter petals about.
> Also in the fall we would carve pumpkins and in No-
> vember we would spread [his grave] with fall leaves
> and in December we would have a tree that we would
> decorate. We would listen to music that made us think
> of him. Like, we'd share headphones when we were
> sitting out there and we would write poetry or letters.
> There is something sacred somehow about it to us,
> like we're creating something or making something

together that is our way to continue to love him, even
in his absence. Remembering him together has been
really life-giving.

Of course, your personal or family ritual doesn't need
to be elaborate. Whether it's making a birthday cake for
your child each year, lighting a candle, and saying "Happy
Birthday," or simply taking some quiet time to reflect on
your child's life and your love for him or her, these remembrances strengthen your child's presence in your life.
Not too long ago, I had a conversation with David, Victor's father. I was moved by what he shared with me:

> On the annual anniversary of Victor's death and on his
> birthday, I make it a special point to sit on a bench in
> my side yard that bears his name, and look through all
> the photos I have of him, bringing back memories of
> him and his life. Usually, on one of those days, I also
> write a letter or poem to him as a way of feeling close
> to him and communicating whatever flows from me. I
> keep those letters and poems in a notebook that I be-
> gan a few weeks after his death. Occasionally, I read
> through what I have written over the thirty-plus years.
> But mostly, I feel peaceful knowing they are there in
> my "Victor Book."

I was touched by David's words and the way he kept
alive his connection to our son. It meant a lot to me to
hear that.

The lovely ways in which parents commemorate the
life and death of their children, whether publicly or pri-
vately, simply or elaborately, could comprise a book in

itself! One father I know always volunteers at a local food kitchen on the day of his son's death. This life-affirming gesture reflects his son's spirit and gives the father a positive focus. Other parents, Susan and Steve, along with their deceased son Gabe's friends and his community, celebrate his birthday with an annual baseball game in his honor. Some parents, such as Sarah, whose daughter Emily died in a car accident at age seventeen, put together commemorative books or websites. In her beautiful book, "Where I Belong: The Selected Works of Emily Shenandoah Brightwood," Sarah included photos of Emily, some of Emily's drawings and writings, and Sarah's own touching words: "Emily, your glow still keeps me warm. Your laughter rings through the house of my longing. I thank you for loving life."

I loved what another mother, Brenda, told me: "On her birthdays, many times, not all twenty, I've done a flower arrangement for church. I like to do it, and there is always symbolism woven into it. Very often I will have five of one kind of flower, whether or not they're noticeable—let's say five white roses in a white bouquet. Nobody else knows that there's one for each year of her life. To me, I get a tickle out of it. I mean, I smile in my heart."

• • •

What do I say when people ask how many children I have?

We had to go to court. In the jury selection a man stood up and, when asked how many children he had, he said, "I have four children. One is in heaven." I liked his present tense of expressing it.

—Jacob, whose twenty-three-year-old son had died in a hit-and-run accident three years earlier

I am Victor's mother as long as I live, not as long as he lived. But how and when to convey this to others can be a tough question. Is it necessary to share something as intimate as your child's death with someone you've just met? Do you want to risk having to answer their questions, hear their well-meaning but unhelpful comments, or worse, have them quickly change the subject? The person may be startled by your response, and you may not want to re-ignite your own feelings or have to take care of the other person's feelings. But if you don't include your child, are you somehow erasing his presence in your life? The simple answer is that your response depends on what you're comfortable with in the moment.

For some, it is an extremely painful question, and they avoid it. I initially interviewed Hedda two months after her twenty-two-year-old son had died suddenly of hepatitis while traveling in Asia, and had the privilege of speaking with her again thirty-two years later. This is what she told me: "My husband and I only went [on travel tours] with the Brits, because Brits do not ask personal questions. Americans are very intrusive. They always ask what do you do and how many kids do you have, and Brits never do that. I never told anybody about my family life, and I could not answer the questions about how many children you have, because if I had to say I had two boys and one died, I think I would just sit there and cry my eyes out. So I couldn't answer those questions. I avoided them."

Others decide how to answer based on the circumstances and how they're feeling. Alan explained it this way: "There's different scenarios. You're on a plane, you're with someone that you're never going to see again, okay, and they ask you how many children you have. You tell them one. You don't start talking about Phillip and bringing that person down and having to go through all the gyrations. Not necessary, not worth it. But if I'm at home and I know it's someone that I'm meeting and I'm going to see [him], yeah, I want to talk about [Phillip] and tell a story and the whole bit."

There were times when I tried answering this question by saying I had two children, but that made me feel I was not honoring Victor's life. It was uncomfortable. It didn't feel good. In fact, it felt like a lie, a silencing, in order not to make others uncomfortable, and I didn't want to feel silenced. As the years have gone by I have become comfortable saying I have three children. Then I wait and see if the person is really interested in asking more. Depending on their sincere interest and my feelings about disclosing myself to them, I decide whether to say anything further. I have found that when answering from the truth of my heart, with someone who really cares to get to know me better, my truth invites them to speak to me about *their* lives, and our relationship deepens.

When I think of my other two children, Andrew and Fay, who are now adults with their own families, I often include Victor in my heart. I still feel that I am the mother of three children. Two are very alive adults living creative and fulfilling lives with their own amazing families, and one died and is with me in spirit. Our relationships continue to change and evolve as we all go through life together and separately, and I guess always will. The love in my heart has expanded as I am blessed with stepchildren, daughters- and sons-in-law, and grandchildren. There is more love, not less.

• • •

HOW DO I HANDLE THE CONTINUING FEELINGS OF GRIEF AND JEALOUSY AS I WATCH MY FRIEND'S CHILDREN GROW?

Even today, when I hear parents talking about children driving them crazy, I bristle. I usually catch myself thinking, "You don't know what crazy is. Crazy is not having your children here at all." At other times I might think, "I wish Krissie were here to drive me crazy."

—Carol, age sixty-eight, whose seven-year-old daughter was swept out to sea by a rogue wave thirty-seven years ago

Waves of sadness often arise when you watch your child's peers growing up, doing those things your child should be doing or that you hoped he would be doing. I remember when the phone rang on New Year's Eve, twelve years after Victor died. I waited for the message, screening my calls. When I recognized Jeff's voice, I immediately picked up the phone. Jeff was Victor's best friend. They went through a lot together and shared so much. Bless his heart; he always calls on important occasions. I feel like his calls are messages from Victor. Jeff had had some hard times but was now working and living with a terrific young woman.

"Hi, Nisha," Jeff said, sounding happy, and I felt relief, knowing he was okay. "Happy New Year! Just want you to be one of the first to know that while we were visiting Diane's father in New York, I asked him for her hand. We are going to be married this summer." There was silence.

I felt breathless; my heart speeded up. *Come on Nisha, you can do it.* "Jeff, congratulations, honey! I am so happy for you. It's great news!" My voice was genuinely enthusiastic. I was not faking it. I was not holding back tears. I was so grateful that I could feel joy for him, though I noticed I was gritting my teeth. I conjured an image of Victor's face, his smile, and with that my jaw relaxed.

"How old are you, Jeff?" I asked.

"Twenty-nine. I was always a little younger than Vic."

I tried to imagine what Victor would have been like at twenty-nine. It's hard to imagine him at any specific age. I can't quite make a picture of him. He seems ageless to me. I see his smiling face and his dimples. What would he be like at thirty, forty, fifty? I thought I would always be asking those questions, if only for fleeting moments, until the day I die. Surprisingly, I no longer imagine what he would be like at different ages and stages of life. He is forever "almost Big 18."

I recognized in that moment that I had come to a place where my memories could be a source of comfort and connection. Many parents mention that even while experiencing pain, over time they feel pleasure remembering their child. You can perhaps now recall a memory of your child without profound grief. You can remember your child, not only with tears, but with smiles.

And if that bug of jealousy and sadness persists, remember you are in charge of what you choose to do. You can be selective about the people you want to be with. If someone repeatedly says or does things that feel insensitive or hurtful, that take you back to a place of pain, you can choose not to continue spending time with that person. Take time alone for yourself or do something special or unusual. It might be as simple as being alone with your thoughts and feelings for a time, turning off your electronic devices, and letting your thoughts wander. Your memories and thoughts cannot be taken away. They are yours for all time, to return to as a touchstone and a source of strength.

...

WHAT IF DEPRESSION AND SADNESS STILL COLOR MY DAYS?

Well, inside of me, there's something dead. I was always a happy person, loving to go. Now I go because I'm sort of pushed into it. And I don't want the rest of my family to feel bad because I feel bad. Something went out of me that never came back. I just don't feel like I ever felt before. I'm not happy about anything, really. There's no joy, really, in things like there used to be.

—Edith, age sixty-six, whose thirty-four-year-old son had died in a pool accident eight years and two months earlier

Of course you still feel sad. And to feel continued difficulty in joining friends or family in their activities is not
uncommon. Grief expert Theresa Rando, PhD, has found
in her research that parents' grief responses tend to be
more intense than those of other mourners. Much other
research confirms that the death of a child produces more
intense grief reactions, greater depression, and sharper anger, guilt, and despair than the loss of a parent or a spouse.

Increasingly, as we've noted, those in the grief community are recognizing that expressions of grief and
mourning vary widely and often follow an oscillating
pattern between feelings of intense loss and the feeling
that something in you is being restored and repaired. We
used to call this "two steps forward, one step back." In
1999, Dutch psychologists Margaret Stroebe and Henk
Schut suggested the term "dual process model" (DPM) to
describe this back and forth. Stroebe and Schut insist that
ups and downs are normal, and grief involves a dynamic
process of oscillation between confronting and avoiding
loss. The swings between feeling grief and moving forward take a huge amount of energy and effort. If you feel
at times that you don't want to deal with your loss or you
want to take a break from focusing on it, that is perfectly
understandable and healthy. This oscillation is the work
of grief.

The question is whether, despite lingering sadness
and depression, you can also feel more positive emotions
beginning to stir within you—the occasional desire to
reengage with others, the ability to find humor in a memory of your child or a comment someone makes, the desire to find renewed meaning in your life. Since parents'

movement through loss and grief is experienced on their own timetable, it's hard to say exactly when these things should happen. One year? Five years? Ten? Ginny offered this estimate: "People who have been through it say it takes three years to be able to breathe and ten years to be able to heal."

Ultimately, you are the best gauge of your own process. If you feel that symptoms of anger, guilt, ennui, agitation, or withdrawal are more ongoing and pronounced than you would like, it could be a sign of what is sometimes called "complicated grief," which is prolonged grief that keeps you from moving forward in your life. It could also be a sign of clinical depression. If you find that your daily life is still severely disrupted or that your relationships with others are suffering, this would be a good time to seek a grief counselor who can lead you through your tangle of emotions. Be sure to find an experienced grief counselor, one who knows how to listen and with whom you feel safe expressing all your feelings, without holding back. A skilled grief counselor can "sit in the fire" with you without judgment, with kindness and compassion.

You can also remind yourself that love and hope are available to you if you let them in. Does it feel dangerous to hope for anything again or to open yourself to love? Love, like rain, does not stop to ask whether or not it is deserved. It may be a baby smiling at you in the market or someone kind enough to hold the elevator for you at work. It may even be someone you love showing you unexpected understanding, even when you're short-tempered or rude in your grief. If love presents itself to you, let it in.

• • •

WHAT WILL STRENGTHEN MY
RELATIONSHIP WITH MY PARTNER NOW?

In many ways it has brought us closer to a point of being
a oneness, but it also made us aware that we are two
individuals with different needs. I learned that, although
we grieve collectively, ultimately, we actually grieve alone.
We've learned how to be sensitive to each other and it
has opened a very honest relationship.

—Gail, age forty-six, whose seventeen-year-old son had died
by suicide four years and eleven months earlier

Now that you are able to stand back a bit from the intense
grief, you may be able to take a clearer look at your relationship with your partner. After the first year, when your
body felt war-torn, and having had more time to heal, you
may be more open to understanding the individual journey of mourning that each of you has had and are continuing to have. Although one or both of you may still require
some form of distance, the ongoing years seem to be the
time when this need for distance subsides and there is renewed interest in the relationship, sexually and emotionally. Of course, this isn't true for everyone, and for some,
the distance between you may persist.

Those relationships that continue to be strong are usually the ones in which partners have been able to understand and accept the differences in the way they grieve.
Carmen reflects back in this way: "Well, just sharing a
horrible tragedy like this, if you can survive each other's
reaction . . . thankfully, I did some reading and I know
that I had to respect [his reaction]." With greater awareness of each other's needs comes a lessening of tension and

a renewed ability to see in your partner the person that you love.

Communication and listening are key. Generally, research shows, those parents who have been able to share their thoughts and feelings with each other feel a stronger bond than those who couldn't. Maureen says, "We didn't talk about it a lot. We didn't talk about it very much at all. That's one of the things that I regret because I feel that I might have been able to help him more if we had been able to talk about it. Because he's not a talker. I'm not a talker, but he's even less of a talker than I am. So I regret that I didn't encourage him to talk more."

It is never too late to renew communication and to let your partner know you are available to talk and to listen. What enables your partner to feel better? A walk? A dinner out? Being busy with other activities? Sex? You and your partner can let each other know what helps the most at this point in time, and what you want from each other. Be ready to understand that you may still not be in sync. But reaching out to each other in small ways can help bring positive feelings to life again. Keep in mind, too, that couples work with a therapist trained in grief can be a positive experience.

• • •

WHAT IS IT LIKE TO BE A SINGLE
BEREAVED PARENT AND THINKING
OF A NEW RELATIONSHIP?

We parted, and I did not have the stamina, I didn't have the
mental stamina, I didn't have the physical stamina to make
a move happen. I didn't have any room to grieve the ending
of that relationship. I was actually quite numb to it. I was
grieving the loss of my son, and nothing trumped that.

—Pamela Ashkenazy, age fifty, whose twenty-year-old
son Daniel had died after a fraternity party in college
eleven years earlier, of a lethal mixture of alcohol
and prescription drugs

My friend Carol was single when her daughter, Krissie,
age seven, was swept out to sea by a rogue wave. A year
later she connected with a man to whom she has now been
married for thirty-seven years. I had a chance to talk with
her husband, Bob, and I asked him what it was like for
him to begin a relationship with someone who was going
through such grief.

Bob said, "I just think you have to open your heart
and participate as much as possible in their process and
honor that process and be willing to give them a lot of
support and recognize that it's something that never goes
away. As Carol describes it, there's a hole in your heart
which gets smaller through the years but never closes up.
And I just think you have to recognize that and grow from
your spouse's relationship with that child and the process
that she or he has to go through with their death, treat it
as a major learning experience for yourself and also an opportunity to support your spouse going through it."

Interestingly, Bob also commented on the fact that when he walked through the door at 5:00 each evening, Carol was able to shift her focus away from the book she was writing about grief so that they could maintain their relationship. It didn't mean that the loss wasn't an ever-present part of their life together or that they didn't talk about it. But Carol made sure that Bob felt that she was turning her energies to her relationship with him in a consistent and positive way.

Victor's father and I divorced in 1983, three years after Victor's death, so I also was single for a number of years and grieving a double loss. I remarried in 2002 and recently asked my husband Steve whether the fact that I was a bereaved mother affected him in any way when he considered marrying me. He was reflective. "It was difficult to see you, someone I love, go through pain. I felt helpless. I wanted to do something, but it soon became apparent to me that there was nothing I could do. There was nothing I could say. I just had to let you go through what you were going to go through and be with you while you were going through it, not try to change you."

He paused. "So I thought, is this something that I want to do, that I want to be a part of? And then I thought about that; I even talked to you about it. I knew that I loved you and wanted to be with you, and this was part of you. If I was going to be with you, I knew that I needed to accept all of who you are."

"Which you've done so beautifully," I said. I was moved by Steve's words. His acceptance and support have been a gift that I appreciate every day. I explored a little further. "What are the positive things for you about being married to me when Victor's life and death is such a part of my life?"

Steve thought for a moment. "Well, Victor is part of your emotional and spiritual life. All that you have experienced makes you who you are. It makes you a deeper, more loving and understanding person."

"Has being with me changed you in any way?" I asked.

"Well, our experience together has changed me. I am more open and I think more caring, more introspective, more spiritual."

I was particularly touched by what Steve had to say about simply being with me in my sadness and grief, not trying to fix things. The idea of acceptance is a powerful one, as is being present with the person you love when they are experiencing a hard time. When we can bring these qualities to our relationship, we encourage love, strengthen understanding, and let each person be who he or she is. If you are single and wondering how a new person will respond to your ongoing process of healing, what better way to open the door to another person than to offer acceptance and seek someone who brings that to you in turn.

And be prepared to recognize that you need more time to heal, to slowly reknit the strands of self, before you'll be ready to launch a new relationship. Hard as this time alone might be, when you feel more solid within yourself, your relationships will have a more solid base as well.

• • •

WHO REMEMBERS MY CHILD?

I was supposed to get my act together. I felt the experience
of the death was discounted by the people around me. I
felt like our family had not dealt with it at all. I would have
loved to have been able to talk with some of his teachers that
had known him. That would have meant a whole lot to me.
But I didn't. I felt like, I don't know, like I wasn't supposed
to or something. I'd like to have heard somebody validate,
some validation of his existence. It was like he hadn't even
existed. In fact, that's how it was coming across.

—Norma, age forty-nine, whose seventeen-year-old son had
died in a sporting accident five years and two months earlier

The issue of being able to talk about your child and remember your child with others is a powerful one that comes up
over and over in my conversations with parents. How can
you go through the process of accepting and integrating
your child's death into your life in a healthy way if you feel
alone with your memories, unable to share them with others? The need to validate your child's vibrant presence in
the world by laughing, crying, remembering, and trading
stories with others is strong and basic. Finding even one
trusted person with whom you can remember a precious
moment or to whom you can relate a true story about your
child is a gift. Says Melanie: "I just don't talk about it with
everybody. But I have several friends who knew her. And I
can still talk about her with them and it's fine."

Often, friends are hesitant to bring up your child's
death, afraid of causing you pain or saying the wrong
thing. Alan says: "I try so hard to tell my friends, 'Don't
worry, there's nothing you can say that's wrong,' but

everyone still—even your best friends—are going to still walk on eggshells and they're going to think hard what comes out of their mouths before they say something." When you let others know that you welcome their memories and thoughts, they may more easily share their stories of your child with you. You can let them know that there is never a time, no matter how many years have passed, when their memories of your child aren't cherished.

It's also possible to share the memory of your child with people who never knew him, so that they can think of him, too. In addition to the bench on Windy Hill that Victor's father David and I established in Victor's name, we also built a picnic table with wheelchair access in the nearby redwood park. We wrote a letter to the people who maintain these memorials, telling them that the memorial bench reflected Victor's love of the outdoors and that the picnic table was intended to enhance others' enjoyment of nature and to reflect Victor's kindness and caring for elders and individuals with disabilities. In our letter, we also told them a little about Victor and said that he is very much loved and missed by his parents, brother Andrew and sister Fay, Uncle Elliott, and his many friends who still contact us to recount their remembrances of him. It felt important to us that the people who tend Victor's memorials should know something about him. It is deeply healing to know that his memory will remain alive in this way.

● ● ●

How do I say good-bye to some old friends and hello to new ones?

They reach a point where there's nothing more your friends can say or do. They have grieved with you, but it has not changed their life. It hasn't changed theirs; it certainly changed mine. Some of my friends, in a very well-meaning way, say, "Oh, Gail, but you've still got so much." And it used to anger me. Nothing takes the place of Mark, and in me is a big emptiness. And darn it, they don't understand.

—Gail, age forty-six, whose seventeen-year-old son had died by suicide four years and eleven months earlier

By the time a number of years have passed, most parents experience a change in the configuration of their friendships. Some friends are better able to handle the manifestations of your grief than others. I have friends who were deeply touched by Victor's death, and I have greatly appreciated their love, concern, and attention. Some were there for me in ways I never imagined possible. However, there will be those who cannot be there for you in the way you'd like because of their own fears, and even long-standing relationships can change drastically. Lu's experience is not uncommon: "We left some friends behind when this happened, that we are no longer seeing or associating with because I guess they couldn't handle us or we couldn't handle them. They tried to pretend everything was normal. And nothing was normal so that ended that." Lu went on to say: "It still makes you angry and hurts you. But people do and I guess it takes a while to learn that they aren't doing it deliberately. That they just don't know what to say and what to do."

The loss of longtime friends is especially hard, and they can't be easily replaced. With time, perhaps you can feel compassion for them in their confusion, appreciate the friendship you did have, and find meaning and connection with others. It is hard not to feel resentful and angry at times when those you thought would be there for you are not, but you will find new friends and sources of support.

My cousin Margery, who is like a sister to me, had a forty-eight-year-old son, Bret, who died on the tennis court of an embolic stroke. Recently, we were talking and she made a point of telling me about "how my circle of people before Bret died has really changed, and now the people that I'm close with are somewhat different, and [I'm] learning to ask for what I need from friends." She told me of one new friend in particular who was interested in getting to know her and hearing about her son. On the anniversary of Bret's birthday, nine years after he died, they went out to lunch together. "And she was just incredibly supportive. And we went to a really nice restaurant that Bret would have liked, and we toasted him, and we ate and we talked and we cried. And I don't have too many people other than you"—she choked up here—"that I can do that with." Of course, I was deeply affected by her words, and I know those feelings so well. How valuable a listening, interested, compassionate friend can be.

Your new life as a bereaved parent can bring with it new and meaningful friendships if you're open to making them, whether through grief support groups, your religious or spiritual community, or activities to commemorate your child, such as fund-raising for a particular cause. In fact, you may not want to turn back to what you had

before. You may find that you have the friends now that
are right for you at this time.

• • •

How have I changed?

I began to validate myself and my own experience. It's
made me a stronger person. I listen to myself more now
and I'm not as easily intimidated. I feel like I [went]
through a concentration camp experience and that's
how I got my strength. Now I want very much to be
a part of this world.

—Norma, age forty-nine, whose seventeen-year-old son had
died in a sporting accident five years and two months earlier

I'll never forget the words of one mother I spoke with.
When I asked her how she felt she had changed, she was
adamant. "I'm sure there are ways that I'm different. I re-
sist that. I don't care what happened; the price was too
great. I'd rather have my child back. And that part of me
says, 'I don't want to have been this person before and become a better person over here, and therefore the price I
needed to pay was the death of my child.'" Tears welled in
my eyes as I told her I felt exactly the same way, and I'm
sure every parent I spoke with would say the same thing
from the bottom of their hearts.

Yet the reality of what happened has thrust us into a
new life. And what I've found is that most bereaved parents in the ongoing years do feel an inner shift, knowing

what they have gone through and reaping wisdom from their experiences. They feel more confident about handling difficult situations, speaking more truthfully and honestly, and putting more trust in following their priorities. You may now walk away from petty or meaningless activities because you have a new respect for life and a better understanding of what a limited time you have on this earth. You might experience yourself as a person more determined to live your life with purpose and meaning. Meg, whose eighteen-year-old daughter had died in a fire eleven years and ten months earlier, put it this way: "When my daughter died, I felt as if everything had been boiled down to the essence. Really boiled down until the dross was out. I guess that's what the empowerment is about. Just the wonderful essence of it all."

You may find yourself much less naive and trusting than you once were, more cautious about what you undertake and who you let into your life. Or perhaps you feel that the veil through which you once viewed the world has been lifted. You see more sharply, more keenly the everyday details around you, the meaning of another person's grimace or the sadness in a neighbor's eyes. You may find yourself feeling a greater connection to nature, appreciating the natural cycles of life, and marveling that life and love exist and persist. "Being in nature, the trees, the ocean, has been so healing," says Jill, whose seventeen-year-old son had died in an automobile accident two years and six months earlier. "It's like a whole new world has opened up to me. I feel like being in it all the time." All of these changes and many others signal that deep reshaping of self that comes with grief.

Most of all, you feel how your grief itself has changed within you. Meg added, "It's strange. I feel whole that I can think about her and feel sad and feel all that love that I have for her. It's a combination of missing her and loving her, and that feels like warm soft salty tears being washed by a warm sea, instead of a cold, jabbing, ripping-apart sea."

If you're sensing changes such as these within yourself, this might be a good time to pay attention. Try this: Write yourself a letter in which you speak to your earlier self, the self you were before your child died, and tell him or her where you are now in your journey forward. What are you now doing that you didn't previously do? Are your interactions with others different in any way? Has your life focus changed? Tell your earlier self everything that is in your heart as you think about how your life feels to you at this moment. Or if you prefer, draw a picture of yourself as you are currently. Notice what you capture and what you leave out. Or talk to your child and share your feelings and your unique journey.

• • •

WILL I BE REUNITED WITH MY CHILD?

Now my connections with Hank are in the spirit, and that
spirit is very much involved with God. I believe that Hank's
spirit continues on and I very much want to believe that. I
don't know if we'll ever be reunited. I have no assurances,
but I do have assurance that he exists, his spirit exists.

—Joyce, age forty, whose thirteen-year-old son had died in a
skiing accident three years and four months earlier

The questions we carry about the afterlife, about what happens to spirit when the body dies, are never more urgent
than in the face of the death of one's child. Death as a con-
crete event, not an abstract idea, has entered your life in the
most piercing way possible. Depending on your beliefs, you
may wonder and reflect on questions of finality, rebirth,
the eternal, and whether a part of the self, in some form,
lives on after physical death. Many parents I spoke with expressed these thoughts and questions. Lu said, "What if I'm
ninety years old when I die? He won't know me in heaven.
Then I thought, *Well, his body isn't going to be up there and my
body isn't. It's going to be our souls or our spirits. So he'll know,
we'll know each other. And we'll be able to greet each other.* That
was a relief. That was an important part that I'd be able to
see him again and we'd know each other."

Margery reflects about her belief in the life of the spirit
this way: "Well, I'm sure this is one of the things that's
helped me survive. I can't imagine going through something like this without some kind of belief that it's not
the end. I mean, that this world is all there was and there
is nothing beyond that. So I know that there are people

who would feel that this was the absolute end. And I can't imagine myself surviving if I felt that way. Death is a passage into another kind of life. I'm sure of that. When my death comes, we will be reunited."

Of course, other parents expressed very different feelings and beliefs. Meg said, "I think a lot of people in a lot of desperate situations need to hang on to something. And I think at that time I needed that belief system. I don't think it was real; I think it was just some kind of solace. When people are dead, they're dead. And that's it. I think I was duped into believing that God was going to take care of me if I did what was right . . . and I think it's a crock. So I have to really be very careful that I don't believe a lot of stuff that is a crock. I believe in the here and now."

I see these questions not as a debate but as a way that we enter into and encounter the awe and mystery of the eternal. The question itself is an opening and, ultimately, an opportunity to make meaning. The reality of your child's death may strengthen your encounter with spirit, and renew your belief in a dimension that is larger than our individual lives. Even if you're left feeling, as Meg did, that "when people are dead, they're dead," that belief raises the challenge and opportunity to make meaning of our lives here in this world. As Rabbi Wolpe wrote, speaking of parents who had lost a child, "The loss could be seen as a sign of meaninglessness, or an opportunity to create meaning. The response to that choice determines the quality, the dignity, and, to some extent, the happiness of our years on earth."

Remind yourself that you are always united with your child, in your heart, in memory, in the remarkable way that your child's spirit remains with you and expresses itself through you. Regardless of your specific beliefs, the questions that you face and your evolving understandings of the miracles of life and death can be a source of meaning and sustenance when seen this way.

• • •

HOW HAVE MY FEELINGS ABOUT DEATH CHANGED?

It made me see how life can change on a dime, you
know, a feather. Just you blink and you could be dead.
So I think I've stepped outside my comfort zone,
instead of keeping my nose to the grindstone and
making a living. I stopped work. I retired. And I
pursued my photography with more passion.

—Margery, age eighty, whose forty-eight-year-old son
had died of an embolic stroke nine years earlier

Many parents report as the years pass that along with a greater appreciation of life, they also feel less fear of death. A bereaved parent once told me that bereaved parents are less afraid to die than any other group of people. Many believe they will be reunited with their deceased child. Others believe that in death, they will be relieved of the pain of missing their child. Others feel that when their child died a part of them already died, so their fear of death dissolved. And some feel that their life on this earth without their child is already too long. In fact, the transformation from the feeling that life will be too long to the feeling that life won't be long enough is one of the signs of healing.

Most people carry a death-denial message that says, *I won't* really *die*. The bereaved know how close life and death are. We are awakened to this reality that others might choose to ignore. Though our awareness is born of deep grief, it can have a positive effect. I spoke with my son Andrew about how his feelings have changed because of Victor's death.

> He's sort of a constant reality check, a reminder that this life is short, that it's precious, and that this is just one aspect of life, this thing that we call living. And death is another aspect of this same thing. It's a very thin veil between what we would call our life and what we call death. So he serves as a reminder of that, which allows me to try to be more willing to go for stuff in my life because why put it off? He serves as a teacher, a reminder, and obviously has influenced a lot how I live my life and my values. I'm always thinking about death and try to be friends with death.

Accepting death in this way can help you to live your life with greater awareness, freedom, and love. When you do not fear death, you are able to take more risks and enjoy life more fully. Far from being morbid, knowing and accepting that we all die someday can reenergize your own love of life. In fact, those who work with the dying often say how alive they feel in the presence of death.

My stepdaughter Kate, a physician, deals regularly with life-and-death situations. She sees firsthand how the development of palliative care and hospice has helped us to better prepare for and accept, rather than ignore or deny, impending death. It has encouraged patients and their families, and all of us, to "be okay with the fact that every-body does die. I think as a culture, we have not accepted that. There are a lot of cultures where death is a very big part of living, as it should be. It's seen as inevitable, but we here in the U.S. have not accepted that." She reflected, though, that palliative care is only an option if death is gradual, from old age or protracted illness. Enduring the trauma and tragedy of sudden death is particularly difficult in a culture that hasn't learned to adequately think about the reality of death.

If you feel you would like to understand more about your feelings about death or want to come to terms with it in a way that you think might strengthen you, there are many workshops available now on death and dying. Con-trary to what you might fear, such workshops tend to be very warm, supportive, positive experiences that bring you closer to yourself, to others, and to those who have died.

• • •

WHAT MAKES MY LIFE WORTH LIVING?

I speak to you, beloved Laure,
Our dancing golden girl with dreams in her curly hair,
Sacrificed by the madness of a predator,
Named for a hero she never got to see,
But brave and wise and beautiful as he.
In your short life on earth you gave such love
That no one whom you knew remained the same.
When doubt and anger prod my mind to pain,
I stop and listen to the You in Me again,

> And try to act as wiser, gentler self,
> Than if I acted for myself alone.
>
> —written by Lillian Kleidman Chodorow, whose twenty-
> one-year-old granddaughter was killed one year and
> seven months earlier

Lori Smallwood Chodorow (also known as "Laure") was killed by a delusional man in May 1980 when she was twenty-one. Her mother, Joan Chodorow, PhD, is a friend and colleague of mine in the dance/movement therapy world. I remember sitting at our kitchen table with Victor after I heard the news, talking about the terrible tragedy and our shock. I remember our conversation so clearly, about how someone can destroy others' lives for no reason and cause so much lifelong sorrow, pain, and loss. I could not have imagined that two months later Victor would die. Some months after Victor's death, Joan visited me and we went into the therapy studio behind my house. Using movement, we supported each other as we expressed our grief. Movement connects immediately and directly to the heart and soul, and is a powerful way to let the grief process move through us. Our time together that day felt sacred.

Nineteen months after Lori died, her grandmother wrote a moving poem in her honor. I've quoted the ending, above, for its beautiful reminder that one of the best ways to honor our loved ones is to "listen to the You in Me again," to act in a way that expresses the best, most loving impulses of our children. In this way we carry forward their legacy and keep their spirit alive in the world. I keep this poem in my mind and heart.

In the face of the incomprehensible, the tragically senseless, the impossible-to-grasp loss, we heal by reaching for these moments of clarity and guidance. Sometimes guidance comes at unexpected times. I remember visiting a friend in a nursing home. We were sitting in a lounge area for all the residents, and my eyes rested on a woman in a pastel print dress. Her white hair was pulled back into a loose knot, and her blue eyes were bright, sparkling, and wise, as if they'd seen two hundred years go by. I wondered how many deaths she had lived through. I found myself imagining what her life might have been like, and then I imagined her speaking to me. This is what she said:

First, let me tell you that you are not alone in your search for answers or reasons. However, the real task is to learn to accept the mystery of it all. You are part of something so huge, so enormous. Can you understand a mountain or an ocean?

I know your heart was broken when your child died, and your spirit was shattered. I, too, experienced that, but it's an illusion. We think there is death. Of course, there is the ending of the physical body, but there is no death of love. Love cannot be drowned, killed, or destroyed. It's only our illusion that it can be. We suffer so when we think we have nowhere to put our love. Your healing has to do with being able to love again. Love yourself, your child, people, animals, nature.

Death and life are not opposites. They are joined by a larger magnificence that holds us all. Your child's death reveals some of the secrets of the universe that only the dead know. Death and life walk shoulder to shoulder, a breath away from each other. But there is a sphere that is neither born nor dies. That essence is what holds us all and accompanies us throughout our births and deaths. It is the greatest mystery of all.

These words echoed within me: "Your healing has to do with being able to love again." I know, of course, that the voice didn't come from the woman I was observing, but from a higher consciousness that lives inside me and will guide me if I am open to it. "You are part of something so huge, so enormous. Can you understand a mountain or an ocean?"

It's a demanding voice. It demands that I risk opening my heart and loving again. It demands that I expand my consciousness to that larger sphere that is not born and does not die. It asks that I see everything in my individual life as part of the larger mystery of all that is. But, I thought in those terrible early days, how can I do this when I am in such pain?

I've found that it takes time to acquire perspective and to see myself as part of a larger whole. It was impossible in the beginning when the loss was so raw. Yet as time passed, this larger view became not only possible, but a source of strength that propelled me to see my life and all my experiences as precious.

I came to know that in the end, daily life and survival are all about love. My love for my son, and the loss that shredded me with pain, were also a doorway to another kind of love, another kind of connection to and communication with my loved ones, alive and dead, and myself.

Having gone through the fire, my heart and consciousness have been expanded. Things that would have bothered me before are minor in comparison to my loss, and they don't upset me anymore. I've grown in compassion for others who are suffering, and I have more to offer to them now. Victor has a different presence in my life than when he was alive. I am at peace with our transformed and loving relationship.

Psychologist and grief expert David Kessler wrote, "Each person finds his or her own personal meaning in bereavement." It is through this individual experience of meaning that you can transform grief "from a cry to a song," as Paula D'Arcy so beautifully expressed in her book, *Song for Sarah: A Mother's Journey Through Grief and Beyond*.

When grief breaks your heart open, it's as if a powerful earthquake has rearranged the landscape around you. You cannot see the world in the same way again. Yet the grief journey through this altered, upturned world can eventually transform pain into a deeper appreciation of the mysteries of life and death, a sense of awe, a sense of purpose and of peace.

May you choose love and life. May you have peace. May you know you are not alone.

We Remember Them

At the rising of the sun and its going down,
we remember them.

At the blowing of the wind and in the chill
of winter, we remember them.

At the opening of the buds and in the rebirth
of spring, we remember them.

At the blueness of the skies and in the warmth
of summer, we remember them.

At the rustling of the leaves and in the beauty
of autumn, we remember them.

At the beginning of the year and when it ends,
we remember them.

As long as we live, they too will live, for they
are now a part of us, as we remember them.

When we are weary and in need of strength,
we remember them.

When we are lost and sick at heart,
we remember them.

When we have joy we crave to share,
we remember them.

When we have decisions that are difficult
to make, we remember them.

When we have achievements that are based
on theirs, we remember them.

As long as we live, they too will live, for they
are now a part of us, as we remember them.

by Sylvan Kamens and Rabbi Jack Riemer
from *The Union Prayer Book*

Appendix A

For Family and Friends:
Wondering What to Do or Say?

May 2016, Tiburon, California

This past month, almost thirty-six years after Victor's death, I was talking with a bereaved father, Bubba, whose thirty-four-year-old daughter had died suddenly from bleeding in her brain stem. He said to me, "You're writing a book. I hope you'll put something in there about the things not to say."

I had to chuckle because I had compiled precisely such a list based on my own experience, and I know many other bereaved parents have done the same.

Bubba went on to tell a story that says it all: "I had one person say, 'Well, you'll get over it,' you know, and . . ."

"But that person had not had a child die," I interrupted.

"No," he said. "And I was talking to a customer of mine, and I told him about this, and he looked at me and he said, 'I had a brother that overdosed.' And his father, who was sitting behind the counter, was eighty-two years old. He stood up and looked at me and tears were in his eyes, and he said, 'Don't ever let anybody tell you you'll get over it.' He said, 'You'll get around it,' he said, 'but you'll never get over it.' And we became instant friends when that man told me that. Instant friends. He said it had been twenty years for him, and he said, 'We still miss him. We still love him.'"

"That sounds like a very wise man," I said.

"But when people say these things, 'Oh, you'll get over it,' you know, they have no idea what's going on, and they're afraid to say anything. They say, 'Well, let's don't talk about that. I don't want you to think about it.' You know, these are things that never leave your mind. It has never ever once left my mind. I've got a picture at the bottom of the stairs so that in the morning the first thing I see when I come down the steps is her picture."

I had a long conversation with Bubba that day, and he said many wise things. "There's a book by Rabbi Kushner," he said, "called *When Bad Things Happen to Good People*. And I met him at the Jewish Book Festival. And he was signing his books and I looked him in the eye, and I said, 'I have a question for you' . . . because his son died at fourteen of a congenital disease . . . 'Were you mad at God?' I just asked him.

"He said, 'Yeah.' And I was surprised he said that. He said, 'What happened to you?' And I told him and he looked at me and he said, 'It's okay to be mad.' He said, 'The mad will go away when the time comes. And don't'—this really surprised me, he said—'don't let anybody talk you out of being mad.'

"But," Bubba went on, "people have no idea what to say to someone who is grieving so badly because they're afraid. They're afraid themselves. It's just the fact they call, and say that, you know, they care. And that to me is so important, that they call. They don't know what to say if they have never been in this situation, especially the ones who have no idea. They have no idea how bad you're hurting. . . ."

Bubba's voice trailed off. Then he said, "There were seven things I wrote down at one time about what you should say or not say." He promised to e-mail them to me, and a few days later his list showed up on my computer.

Bubba's suggestions for what not to say:

"Grieving people don't need these remarks:
They are in a better place.
I would just kill myself.
You'll get over it.
I would die.
Try not to think about it.
I know how you must feel.
You have other children."

And here are my own suggestions!

• • •

Should I call? How do I know what would be most helpful?

By all means call or send a note. It's common to feel that you don't know what to do or say. No one does. You can tell your friend that you would like to support him and ask him for specific ways you can be of help. Believe what he tells you in that moment and continue to ask for an update. Understand that he may or may not know what to ask for or feel able to ask. Offer some specific suggestions. Can you help with the practical tasks that have to be accomplished, such as shopping for groceries, bringing meals, or posting messages on social media? If there are other children, can you help by giving them rides or taking them to the park? Can you help with plans for the memorial service or go with your friend on a difficult errand, such as choosing a memorial plaque? I still remember how grateful I was when my dear friend Lee organized a notebook for my thank-you notes I wanted to send but had no energy or brain power to deal with.

One mother I spoke with put it this way: "I think the worst thing people can do at this kind of time is give advice because they don't really know, they haven't been through it. And I think that the best thing they can do is not talk a lot at all and just kind of let the person take the lead. I think being nurturing is good, so you know, 'Can I do something for you?'" I heard similar comments over and over from bereaved parents, that those who sat with them in compassionate silence, who listened or simply walked alongside them in their grief, were giving an invaluable gift. Your consistent, loving presence is what's most important. Your look, your touch will tell your friend that you care. As one bereaved mother wisely observed, "Walking with someone rather than showing them the way is the true essence of friendship." It's also the best way to support the bereaved.

What do grieving people say helps the most?

When this question comes up, the answer most often given by those in grief is that the most valuable and nourishing thing friends and family can do is to listen. It is not an easy thing to sit with someone you care about or love and hear their pain, grief, or fear. It takes courage to just listen, not interrupt, not bring forth your own ideas and advice. I remember my close friend Patricia extending this kind of loving "deep listening" to me when I was in intense grief. She was able to listen attentively, with a compassionate, open heart, with love and faith that things would get better. This kind of listening gives the message, "I love you. I am here for you. Even though I wish with all my heart that there was something I could do to make your pain go away, I will not try to fix you or make you better. I will hold you in my heart, in my love." Writer and physician Rachel Naomi Remen has said, "The most basic and powerful way to connect to another person is to listen. Just listen. Perhaps the most important thing we ever give each other is our attention. A loving silence often has far more power to heal and to connect than the most well-intentioned words."

Sometimes people express a hesitancy to listen in this way, perhaps because they fear being sucked into someone's grief. It's true that this kind of listening can be hard, and if you find over time that it becomes draining, it's important to set limits so that you don't become resentful. For instance, if your friend wants to talk on the phone, you might say, "Now doesn't work for me, but may I call you in an hour?" Or "I have fifteen minutes right now and

I would love to spend them with you on the phone if this
works for you."

Should I continue to write notes or
call even if I don't hear back?

By all means continue to leave a phone message, send an
e-mail, or write notes. Especially as the weeks and months
pass by, it is so important to stay in touch. Don't disappear! Sending a note from time to time to let your friend
know that you're thinking of her is a supportive thing to
do. What's important is that you not ask your friend for
her time and energy if she is not ready to reach out to others. Simply let her know that your heart is with her and if
there's a specific way that you can be of help, to please let
you know. One mother said, "I had friends that wanted to
help out, and I'm like, 'If you can just make food and bring
it over that would be great.' But I didn't need to speak to
them. I didn't want to speak to them. I told them, we told
everybody, we didn't know when we would be back in
contact." It's common to need some "space" from friends
and family members in order to grieve. Let your bereaved
friend know that you will be there to listen and help however you can when she is ready.

What can I say that won't sound like a cliché?

Yes, it's a good idea to avoid those clichés! Here are some
of the frequently used ones and some good alternatives:

"I know how you feel." (No one can know this. Even those who have lost a child cannot, since each loss is different for each individual.) Instead, be honest about your feelings. Say you don't know what to say; you can't imagine what it's like; you don't have words to express yourself. Most important, tell her, "I am so sorry. I am here for you." Or, "I'm so sorry for your loss."

"God only takes the good ones." "It was his time to go." "He's in a better place." (There is never a right time or a right reason for a child to die.) Instead, you can support your friend by accepting his pain, tears, confusion, sadness, and anger. Let him know it is understandable to have all those feelings and more.

"You'll get over it." (She won't. Some aspects of the loss continue forever.) Instead, let her know that the death of her child is important to you. Tell her, "We loved [name of child] so much," or "[child's name] is always in my thoughts." Listen with compassion to whatever she needs to express.

"You look good; you must be feeling better." (How she looks on the outside and how she feels on the inside are two different things.) Instead, simply offer a hug, a touch. Say "I'm so glad to see you."

Are there certain words or phrases I should use or not use when referring to my friend's child's death?

This question is so important because how we use language matters to most parents whose child has died. For example, many parents are sensitive to the way the death of their child is described. Many suicide parents urge people to use the phrase "died by suicide" rather than "committed suicide" with its echo of someone committing a crime. In this case, changing our language can help reduce stigma. One mother found "She took her own life" to be preferable to "She committed suicide" because "took her own life" implied that her child had made a decision and suggested an act that required a certain strength.

Of course, you can't be expected to know precisely what words to use or not use. It is always wise and caring to ask parents if they prefer to use certain words rather than others when referring to their child's death. Or you can simply follow their lead and use the language that they use. Let them know that you are prepared to respect their feelings in this regard and that you understand that one's choice of language can carry particular and important meanings.

Should I talk about my friend's child when I'm with her?

Yes, by all means talk about your friend's child with her. Don't hesitate to mention her child's name in your conversations or to comment on any displayed photos. Sharing your own memories of her child and listening to her memories is healing and supportive. She needs to process her feelings of pain to resolve them. Follow her lead and listen to what she is saying. Ask questions and clarify your understanding of her feelings. She knows what she wants to say and when she wants to talk about her experience and her dead child.

If you are in doubt about how she feels when you speak about her child, ask her. "Are you okay with my talking about [child's name] now?" A father I spoke with described his friends that were most helpful: "They were there when we needed them, didn't push, but kept following up with us, willing to talk about whatever we wanted to talk about, talk about Michael when the time was right. I think friends have to let you talk and discuss whatever you want to, whether you want to talk about your child or whether you don't want to talk about your child at certain times, they have to go by your lead. And they can't shy away from you when you need them." Sage advice.

Should I remember my friend's child's birthday as I always did?

Yes, don't hesitate to remember your friend's child's birthday or death day with a call, a card, or a special memory or poem. She will welcome knowing that others have not forgotten her child and are thinking of her. One mother I spoke with said: "One of my really good friends did something on Shana's birthday, and I'm like, this is the best thing that anyone has ever done for me. She sent me this beautiful e-mail and it talked about Shana. It was just like a few sentences about Shana being such a compassionate, loving soul and her brown sparkling eyes. There was something else she said; it was so Shana, and she knew my daughter so well. I e-mailed her back and I said, 'That was the most beautiful thing that you could do for me today.'"

What if I'm finding my friend's emotions
to be too overwhelming?

The feelings of grief *are* overwhelming, and it's not surprising that you might be feeling that way. If you are, the
best thing you can do is to be honest about how you're
feeling, with yourself as well as your friend. You might
say, "Your feelings are completely understandable, and I
can't imagine how difficult this is for you. I love and care
about you, but this conversation is bringing up some difficult feelings for me right now. I want to continue to be
here for you, but I need to take some time to think about
what that's about." Keep in mind that painful as grief is,
it's a growth opportunity as well, for the grieving person
and for those touched by the grief of others.

What if I think my friend is not recovering
as fast as he should, or that he needs to
think about other things?

Each person's way of dealing with the death of a child is
unique, and there are no specific time schedules for grief
or recovery. Let your friend know that you understand
that the ongoing process of healing takes a lot longer than
you or she would like it to, and that you will stay with her
through this process. As time passes, understand that her
sense of loss and missing her child will always be there.
Some aspects of grief can increase before they get better, such as the need to continue remembering her child,
and some never change, such as the sense that there is a
large, painful hole in her life. Understand that she has been

changed by her experience, and she will not be her "old self" in the same way again.

Should I make suggestions for things that might help my friend cope, such as a book to read or a grief group?

Providing a list of bereavement resources—several titles of books, a list of telephone numbers and addresses of support groups such as the local chapter of The Compassionate Friends, websites that provide online support—is a helpful gesture. (See the Resource List in the back of this book.) Not everyone is aware of the many resources available to bereaved parents. Tell your friend you want her to have the list should she feel ready at some point to look into these resources. Honor her response, and let her know that you understand that she will have her own sense of whether or not, and when, these resources may feel right for her. Understand that she may have no energy to pursue these leads, and offer to make calls for her or to do research on-line to find information that could be helpful to her.

My friend is drinking more than usual (eating too much, has stopped exercising, etc.), but how can I bring that up at a time like this?

These are tough questions that reflect a difficult situation. If you have any of these concerns, I recommend getting the advice of a therapist who specializes in supporting the bereaved. Even one meeting with a knowledgeable grief therapist can provide valuable insight and direction and help you know how to address your concerns. Refer to the Resource List in the back of this book for ideas about where to start.

What if I'm worried for my friend's well-being?

Despairing, even suicidal thoughts are not uncommon in the face of shattering loss. It is rare that a bereaved parent will actually die by suicide, but depression can be an ongoing weight, coloring your friend's days for months, even years at a time. Most often depression lifts slowly and naturally over the course of the first two to five years after the death of a child. What you can do is to be patient and understand that your friend is taking the time he needs to heal. Simply being with him—sitting quietly or taking a walk, bringing a take-out meal or listening while he re- members his child—without asking that he be his old self is a wonderful gesture of friendship. If you feel that your friend is at risk for self-harm or is unable to function well, please consult a grief therapist to get more specific insight into how you might help.

What if I'm feeling distant or unable to really connect?

It's not unusual for friendships to shift or become strained or even to end because of the changes and stress brought about by grief. This is a time for you to reevaluate what this friend means to you, whether you can continue being a valued friend, and if so, how. It can be helpful to read books on bereavement or go online to find out more about the grief process. The Suggested Reading in Appendix B at the back of this book can be useful to friends and family as well as bereaved parents. Having a fuller understanding of what your friend is dealing with may strengthen your feelings of support and compassion.

How long will my friend grieve?

As time passes, the pain and devastation become less acute, but they do not disappear. Your friend is still hurting. Your understanding and acknowledgment of his ongoing sadness is helpful and empathetic. When you listen to your friend and try to understand as best you can your friend's ongoing grief process, you are providing invaluable support. Recognizing grief as a lifelong, evolving process, different for each person, will help your friend to feel cared for and understood.

Appendix B

Suggested Reading

Apple, Dennis L. *Life After the Death of My Son: What I Am Learning*. Kansas City, MO: Beacon Hill Press, 2008.

Bonanno, George A. *The Other Side of Sadness: What the New Science of Bereavement Tells Us About Life After Loss*. New York: Basic Books, 2009.

Boorstein, Sylvia. *Happiness Is an Inside Job: Practicing for a Joyful Life*. New York: Ballantine Books, 2008.

Chodron, Pema. *When Things Fall Apart: Heart Advice for Difficult Times*. Boulder, CO: Shambhala, 2000.

Christina, Greta. *Comforting Thoughts About Death That Have Nothing to Do with God*. Charlottesville, VA: Pitchstone Publishing, 2014.

Deits, Bob. *Life After Loss: A Practical Guide to Renewing Your Life After Experiencing Major Loss*. Boston: Lifelong Books, 2009.

Doka, Kenneth J. *Grief Is a Journey: Finding Your Path Through Loss*. New York: Atria Books, 2016.

Feigelman, William. *Devastating Losses: How Parents Cope with the Death of a Child to Suicide or Drugs*. New York: Springer Publishing, 2012.

Fine, Carla. *No Time to Say Goodbye: Surviving the Suicide of a Loved One.* New York: Random House, 1999.

Frankl, Viktor E. *Man's Search for Meaning: An Introduction to Logotherapy.* Boston: Beacon Press, 2006.

Gilbert, Allison. *Passed and Present: Keeping Memories of Loved Ones Alive.* Berkeley, CA: Seal Press, 2016.

Horsley, Gloria, and Heidi Horsley. *Open to Hope: Inspirational Stories of Healing After Loss.* Palo Alto, CA: Open to Hope Foundation, 2011.

Jamison, Kay Redfield. *Night Falls Fast: Understanding Suicide.* New York: Alfred A. Knopf, 1999.

Kornfield, Jack. *A Path with Heart: A Guide Through the Perils and Promises of Spiritual Life.* New York: Bantam Books, 1993.

Kübler-Ross, Elisabeth, and David Kessler. *Life Lessons: Two Experts on Death and Dying Teach Us About the Mysteries of Life and Living.* New York: Scribner, 2014.

Kushner, Harold S. *When Bad Things Happen to Good People.* New York: Anchor Books, 2004.

Levine, Peter. *In an Unspoken Voice: How the Body Releases Trauma and Restores Goodness.* Berkeley, CA: North Atlantic Books, 2010.

Nhat Hanh, Thich. *Anger: Wisdom for Cooling the Flames.* New York: Penguin, 2002.

Parnell, Laurel. *Transforming Trauma: EMDR—the Revolutionary New Therapy for Freeing the Mind, Clearing the Body, and Opening the Heart.* New York: W. W. Norton, 1997.

Sprague, Zander. *Making Lemonade: Choosing a Positive Pathway After Losing Your Sibling.* San Francisco: Paradiso Press, 2013.

Wolpe, Rabbi David. *Making Loss Matter: Creating Meaning in Difficult Times.* New York: Riverhead Books, 2000.

Wray, T. J. *Surviving the Death of a Sibling: Living Through Grief When an Adult Brother or Sister Dies.* New York: Three Rivers Press, 2003.

Appendix C

Resource List

Types of Loss by Category

Accident

All Resources are national or international unless specified as a specific regional resource.

- Mothers Against Drunk Driving, madd.org: Works to end drunk driving, help fight drugged driving, support the victims of these violent crimes, and prevent underage drinking.
- The Drowning Support Network, drowningsupportnetwork.wordpress.com: A peer support group for people who have lost loved ones in drownings or other aquatic accidents.

Addiction/Overdose

- 129 a Day, 129aday.org: An advocacy group offering resources and support for those who have lost a loved one to drug overdose.
- Alcoholics Anonymous, AA.org: An international fellowship of men and women who have had a drinking problem.

- Al-anon Families, al-anon.org: A group that nurtures strength and hope in friends and families of problem drinkers.
- Center for Open Recovery, openrecoverysf.org (San Francisco Bay Area): Champions long-term recovery by ending the stigma of addiction and offers support and resources.
- Food Addicts in Recovery Anonymous, foodaddicts .org: An international fellowship of men and women experiencing difficulties in life due to food obsessions.
- Narcotics Anonymous, na.org: Helps people find a way out of drug addiction.
- Tim Griffith Foundation, timgriffithfoundation.org (San Francisco Bay Area): Provides services to those experiencing addiction, violence, and loss.

General
- Alive Alone, alivealone.org: An organization that educates and financially supports bereaved parents who have lost their only child or all their children.
- Association for Death Education and Counseling, adec.org: A professional association for grief counselors and others in the field. Offers a current list of certified grief counselors as well as other information.
- Elisabeth Kübler-Ross Center Foundation, ekrfoun dation.org: An organization inspired by psychiatrist Elisabeth Kübler-Ross, death and dying and hospice pioneer.
- National Organization for Victim Assistance, trynova .org: Champions dignity and compassion for those harmed by crime and crisis.

Grief Support

- Bereaved Parents USA, bereavedparentsusa.org: A national nonprofit self-help group that offers support, understanding, compassion, and hope, especially to the newly bereaved.
- Center for Complicated Grief, Columbia University School of Social Work, complicated grief.org: For some people, feelings of loss are debilitating and don't improve even after time passes. In complicated grief, painful emotions are so long-lasting and severe that the bereaved has trouble accepting the loss and resuming life.
- The Compassionate Friends, compassionatefriends .com: The largest nondenominational international organization that provides grief support after the death of a child. Transforming the pain of grief into the elixir of hope. Local meetings throughout the United States and internationally. The Marin Chapter meets every third Monday in Novato, California at 7:30 p.m. See www.tcfmarin.org, 415-457-3123.
- Dougy Center, dougy.org: A safe place where children, teens, young adults, and their families grieving a death can share their experiences.
- EMDR International Association, emdria.org: Advances the education, practice, and science of EMDR therapy for trauma.
- Grief Beyond Belief, Griefbeyondbelief.org: Faith-free support for nonreligious people grieving the death of a loved one.
- Grief Net, grief.net: Support for persons dealing with grief, death, and major loss.

- Grief Share, griefshare.org: A Christian organization that offers seminars and support groups led by people who understand grief.
- Jewish Healing Center, www.jewishhealingcenter .org: Focuses on the Jewish spiritual experience with regard to medical care and bereavement. Sponsors a "Grief and Growing" healing weekend in the San Francisco Bay area, but all bereaved individuals and families are welcome.
- Kara, Kara-grief.org (Palo Alto, CA): With empathy as its focus, Kara compassionately serves the grieving, from children through adults. Kara also hosts Camp Erin, a free weekend grief camp designed for children ages six to seventeen who have experienced the death of a family member or friend.
- Loss of a Twin, Twinlesstwins.org: A safe and compassionate community for twinless twins to experience healing and understanding.
- MISS Foundation, www.missfoundation.org: Online support group and resources for families after the death of an infant or child. Also sponsors the Kindness Project, a program utilizing kindness cards to honor random acts of kindness while venerating the memory of a deceased child.
- National Alliance for Grieving Children, national allianceforgrievingchildren.org: Provides information and referral to families victimized by homicide.
- Open to Hope Foundation, opentohope.com: Most-visited grief and loss website on the Internet. Helps people find hope after loss.
- Project Grace, project-grace.org: A group dedicated to providing a unique and transformative option

for persons suffering from the loss of a child. Sutter
Health Grief and Bereavement Support, suttercareat
home.org/griefsupport/ (Northern California): Offers
individual and group support before and after a loss
and designs educational programs for businesses and
schools.

Illness

- American Hospice Foundation, americanhospice
  .org: Provides links to many hospice, caregiving, and
  grieving resources on the Internet.
- Candlelighters Childhood Cancer Foundation, candle
  lighters.org: Educates, supports, and serves children
  with cancer and their families.

Murder

- Contra Costa Crisis Center, crisis-center.org/ (San
  Francisco Bay Area): Its mission is to keep people
  alive and safe, help them through crises, and connect them with culturally relevant resources in the
  community.
- Hospice by the Bay, hospicebythebay.org (San Francisco Bay Area): Offers bereavement counseling and
  bereavement support groups for parents and others
  who have lost loved ones.
- Mothers of Murdered Sons and Daughters, moms
  .memorial-of-love.net: A grief site and message board
  for mothers to communicate with other mothers and
  share their grief.
- Mothers Against Murder, mothersagainstmurder.org:
  Provides support to silently grieving families of murder victims.

- Parents of Murdered Children, pomc.com: Support group for anyone who has lost someone due to homicide.
- Tragedy Assistance Program for Survivors, taps.org: A national nonprofit organization made up of, and providing services to, all those who have lost a loved one on active duty with the armed forces.

Neonatal

- American SIDS Institute, sids.org: An organization dedicated to prevention of sudden infant death and the promotion of infant health.
- Brief Encounters, briefencounters.org: Support groups for parents whose babies have died before, during, or after birth.
- Helping After Neonatal Death, handonline.org: Helps parents, their families, and their health care providers cope with the loss of a baby through stillbirth, miscarriage, or SIDS or other causes after pregnancy. Even though its headquarters are in California, it can be useful to others nationally.
- MEND, mend.org/infant-loss-organizations/, Helping Hand After Neonatal Death (HAND): Reaches out to families who have lost a baby. Support groups exist in California. It can connect others to support groups nationally.
- International Stillbirth Alliance, stillbirthalliance.org: Helps parents cope with stillborn and infant death.
- National Share, nationalshare.org: Offers support for pregnancy and infant loss.

Self-Help
- The Centering Corporation, centering.org, and www .griefdigestmagazine.com: Has provided education and resources for the bereaved since 1977. Thousands of grief resources for children and adults.

Suicide
CRISIS HOTLINE INFORMATION

- 24/7 Suicide Prevention Lifeline, suicideprevention lifeline.org, 800–273–8255, or call 911.
- Suicide Hotline, 800–Suicide
- Depression and Crisis Hotline, 800–784–2433
- National Institute for Trauma and Loss in Children (TLC), 877–306–525
- National Center for Victims of Crime, victimconnect .org: Offers confidential referrals for crime victims, 855–4–VICTIM.
- National Hispanic Resource Hotline, 800–473–3003
- American Association of Suicidology, www.suicidol ogy.org: Information, support, and resources for suicide loss survivors.
- American Foundation for Suicide Prevention, afsp .org: An organization that funds research about suicide, informs the public about and advocates for suicide prevention, and supports those affected by suicide.
- Friends for Survival, friendsforsurvival.org: Support for those grieving the suicide death of a family member or friend.

- ReachOut, reachout.com: Tells the stories of those dealing with a variety of mental health issues or who are otherwise trying to "get through tough times"; also provides forums; 800-448-3000.
- Survivors of Suicide, survivorsofsuicide.com: An organization for families and friends of suicide victims.

Endowments, organizations, and special projects founded in memory of their children by parents interviewed for this book.

- An Artists Retreat with Anna Rhodes, anartistsretreat.com: Created in honor and memory of Anna Rhodes's son, Nathaniel, this is a concentrated art course taught in extraordinary settings, bringing together participants from around the world.
- Beyond Differences, beyonddifferences.org: This national organization based in the San Francisco Bay Area and created in memory of Lili Rachel Smith works to inspire students at middle schools nationwide to end social isolation and create a culture of belonging for everyone.
- Franklin Micah Wood Endowment, foundation.seattlecentral.edu/: "We established this endowment because we had hopes that one day Franklin would get a degree in graphic design. Franklin was killed before he could make that decision. Our hopes did not die with him. This endowment provides scholarships for students seeking degrees in graphic design, photography, or apparel design."

- Gabe Bouchard Foundation, GabeBouchardFound
  ation.org: In memory of Gabe Bouchard, this foundation provides compassionate, life-saving support and
  information for youth struggling with the disease of
  addiction, their families, and the community.
- Michael B. Zalkin Endowment, tip.duke.edu/about
  /giving/donor-honor-roll: In honor of Michael
  Zalkin, who had qualified for this program, the endowment pays for six to eight students to attend the
  summer Duke Tips programs at universities across the
  country.
- The Philip Michael Silverman Memorial Endowment
  Fund etzchaim.net/secure/fund donations: Among
  other things, it pays for tutors in the education depart-
  ment and sponsors the It Won't Happen to Me Driving Program (iwhtm.org) and Teen Victim Impact
  program (TVIP) so participants can attend free.
- Sacred Doors of Atlanta, www.Margerydiamond
  photography.com: A special photographic project de-
  picting twelve congregational ark doors. Margery Diamond says, "It is filled with my dreams for creating
  a fine art photography piece to honor my son Bret's
  memory.
- *Where I Belong*, an anthology of the writing and artwork of Emily Shenandoah Brightwood, 1997–2015,
  by Sarah Livia Brightwood, emilybrightwood.com:
  You can view the entire book or download it for free
  from the website.

Gratitudes

During the past thirty years, many hearts, hands, and spirits have helped this book become what it is. It really is "our" book. I wish I could list each person by name who has impacted this book and my life during all these years, but space won't allow that.

I have always believed that to know about grief, we must listen to the voices of the bereaved. Every time this book became too hard to write, I was inspired to continue as I remembered the seventy-eight bereaved parents and family members who so generously shared their intimate stories in the hope that their journeys would help others. To each of you, thank you with all my heart for allowing me the privilege of knowing your child and sharing your love, grief, and wisdom. This book could not have been created without your trust and your open hearts. I wish I could have included each deeply touching and profound interview in its entirety. Please know that whether or not you are specifically mentioned in these pages, your contribution has been valuable and essential to this book. I felt a special and sacred bonding when we talked, and you and your child are etched in my heart forever. I hope our time together also served as a place and a time for you to continue your healing. To my clients over the years, you have my deepest appreciation for your trust and the privilege of witnessing your journeys of grief and healing.

To my publisher, John Radziewicz, and the dedicated and talented team at Da Capo Lifelong Press, I know I have been in the best of hands and am so deeply grateful. My heartfelt thanks to editor Renee Sedliar, who "got" my book from the beginning. You were collaborative and encouraging but like a laser in your wise edits. To have an editor who so deeply understood the essence of this book with your compassion and wisdom was a bountiful gift. My appreciation to Miriam Riad, Renee's assistant, for your enthusiasm for this project. Your indispensable behind-the-scenes work kept things moving smoothly. Thank you to project editor Michael Clark for shepherding the manuscript through production with great care and attention to detail, and for being such a superbly professional and organized partner in this process. To Beth Partin, thank you for your amazing eagle eye and experienced copyediting, which is something of a lost art. To Alex Camlin, creative director, my appreciation for your patience and creative input. To publicist Raquel Hitt and marketing director Kevin Hanover and his team, a huge thank-you for the most important task—making sure this book reaches the people for whom it is written.

To my agent Felicia Eth, who saw what this book could be and was willing to take a risk with a first-time author, my deep appreciation for your shrewd business acumen, good advice, and follow-through. I feel as though I won the agent lottery. Thank you.

To editor Dorothy Wall, thank you for becoming a dear friend who understood my heart, my voice, and the vision of this book. You wholeheartedly contributed your writing and editing skills, compassion, and expertise. You have been the perfect collaborator for me and for this book and have made the difficult task of writing about a painful subject absolutely joyful. Your influence appears on every page, and I can say without hesitation that I could not have done this without you.

To my family, lifelong friends, and new friends who lovingly contributed to my Kickstarter campaign or made private individual gifts, thank you for your generous financial assistance. Without your amazing belief in this book, it would still only be a dream. I am eternally grateful to each of you. Thank you to Ed Dudkowski, videographer par excellence, and Suzanna Gratz, for kick-starting my Kickstarter campaign, and Joe Preis, for saving the day with his computer magic.

I have been blessed with so many friends and family who have given their time and love to ensure that this book was completed. You have all lovingly sustained me on this lifelong journey of healing through the tears and loss, joy and growth. As I compile this bounty of names, I realize again how fortunate I am to be surrounded by so much remarkable support. Thank you for your unrelenting faith and for being by my side and in my heart during my healing and the writing of this book. It is an impossibility to name everyone who graciously touched my life and offered encouragement during this incredible process. To anyone unnamed, my apologies and gratitude to each of you.

Early in my writing process I was bolstered by many talented helpers. Thank you to Lara Owen, Victoria

Zackheim, and David Colin Carr, who put their hands on the earliest incarnation of the manuscript and believed in this project. To Nina Solomita, thank you for your courage and sensitivity in editing yet another early version of the manuscript. Thank you to Ronda Dave Tycer for your essential contributions to my early research, valuable direction, and enthusiasm. To Helene Larson, my gratitude for parachuting in to help with the initial draft of the proposal and for your excellent editing and humor. To Nancy Fish, marketing maven and my "fairy godmother" who was available to answer my questions, I'm deeply grateful for your advice and counsel and for encouraging me over hurdles with wisdom, compassion, and humor. Thank you to all my advance readers for taking the time out of your busy lives to read the complete manuscript and to the people who so graciously endorsed my book. You have my deepest appreciation.

Thank you to Book Passage for being a special, cozy place where books and authors still matter. I am grateful to Sam Barry and the "Path to Publishing" program for your professional expertise; to Kathy Ellison for excellent editing suggestions; and to mentor Melissa Cistaro for your kindness, wisdom, and generous guidance. My appreciation to Cara Gluck and Book Passage for hosting my book launch.

To my friend Peggi Johnson, thank you for your eye for detail and valuable information and keeping me informed. My appreciation to Brenda Knight for your publishing consultation, PR suggestions, and insight; to Isabel Allende for your input on my title; and to Susan Gordon for insisting I read every word of the manuscript out loud to you and for your suggestions. To Alice B. Acheson, thank you for your informative class on publishing, and accept my deepest gratitude for introducing me to Dorothy Wall.

To Lilly O'Brien, thank you for connecting me to BAIPA and for introducing me to your husband, Jim O'Brien, the best ever Mac tech person with the patience of a saint. To Sally Wiatrolik, thank you for office support, patience, and kindness. Thank you to Laurel Hilton for your research skills, PR and marketing acumen, and commitment to this project, and to Shelley Chance for your excellent transcriptions of my interviews. To both of you, my appreciation for your compassion working with sensitive material.

My gratitude to Dr. Katie Rodan and Dr. Kathy Fields for your devotion to changing lives. Thank you to my Rodan+Fields family, and my deep appreciation to my R+F soul sisters for your generosity and help spreading the word. Thank you to my 12-step fellows for your love and inspiration each step of the way.

I'm blessed to have many loving cousins. A huge hug of appreciation to each of you for your love and support. Thank you to Jane Slotin for your early interest and belief in this book and for generously introducing me to Nan Satter, who introduced me to Toni Poynter, whose remarks encouraged me to keep going; to Nancy and Leon Slotin, for being our family historians; to Marcy Lindgren, for sharing your organizational skills and cheering me on; to Deb Jospin, for your experience as an author; to Margie Diamond, for being the sister I never had while walking every step of the way through tears and laughter and

encouraging me to "finish this book!"; to Kathy and Ar-
thur Rettig, for always remembering the important dates
and giving me unwavering love and encouragement; to
Harriet Simmons, for your amazing knowledge and suggestions, to Jed Simmons, for your strong words of support, and to Jeanne Shaw, for your guidance from afar.
Thank you to my uncles, Dr. Milton Mazo, who knew the
sorrow of bereaved families and dedicated his life to saving
children, and Billy Poole, who showed me life is worth
celebrating even in times of sadness.

A heartfelt thank-you to Sarah Brightwood for your
support and generous hospitality; to Lolly Font, yoga guru
and Italian chef par excellence; to Jeanne Lythcott for your
wisdom and friendship through many lifetimes; to Davida
and Alvin Deutsch for your caring and visits to California;
to Hilary Mandel for your compassion for the bereaved
and for starting a sibling grief support group; to Lee Pollak
for the grief and joy we have shared through the years; to
Pamela Ashkenazy for your bereaved support groups and
for your research on mother's grief; to Carol Kearns for
setting the example and leading the way; and to Patricia
Spinoza, for sisterhood, your joy, and shamanic gifts.

My appreciation to new friends, lifelong friends, and
extended family, some of whom are mentioned here for
offering encouragement and support, each in your own
unique way: Gail Adler, Pamela Aparicio, Dennis Apple,
Oran Arazi-Gamliel, Lane Arye, Bill Bain, Bernie and
Doug Beck, Karl Bednarek, Ruth Bell, Mary Ann and
Steve Benedetti, Linda and Chuck Bergman, Bob Bing-
ham, the BLE community, William Bratter, Mimi and
Sheldon Breiner, Jayne Brodie, Lori Bush, John Caple,

Kris Carlson, Angel Castillo, Diana Chiarabano, Marjo-
rie Clark, the Compassionate Friends Community, Amy
Cooper, Judy Domenici, Victoria Elbrecht, Daniel Ellen-
berg, Laurie Engle, Ginny Felch, Prudy Ferrone, Mei Ling
Fong, Rose Gallo-Rojas, Genesse Gentry, Willie Gordon,
Ursula Hohler, Gloria Horsley, Kristin Jakob, Kurt Jor-
dan, Christa Kaufmann, Mona Khashoggi, Michael Kil-
groe, Feather and John King, Char Knox, Sapphire Kohl,
Alan Kolsky, Susan Levin, Christopher Levy, Erin Linn,
Marti London, Vicki Longoria, Paul Macomber, Master-
mind Mavens, Lo Anne Mayer, Rita Melconian, Lauren
Mescon, Flo and John Mizell, Dana Oliver, Andrew Oser,
Suzy Piallat, Rita Piazali, Carolyn Preis, Rabbi Jackie
Redner, Mark Renneker, Janet Roberts, Norma and Alex
Robichek, Sue Robichek, Nancy Saltzman, Cintia Van
Sambeek, Sandra Samuels, Susie Sheftel, Bonnie and Alan
Silverman, Ace Smith, Angela Soper, Lois Stark, Sun-
flower Wellness, Abro Sutker, Ed Talmus, Laura Talmus,
Susan Talon-Mazer, Bubba Taratoot, Monica and Stephen
Wood, Andy Zalkin, Leslie Zann, and Theresa Ziskovsky.

To Judi Bell, there from the beginning, who stood by
me with unconditional love, thank you for your big heart,
wisdom, and guidance through all these years. Your hugs
nourished me. To Patricia Savitri Burbank, who suggested
I write about the things I did not want to remember, my
deepest gratitude for your continued sisterly love, for always
being there for me, and for your compassion and wise presence in my life. To Katie Hendricks, who helped me take
my first deep breath after Victor died, thank you for your
loving friendship, generous support, and humor. To Anna
Rhodes, thank you for being family, for your passion and

loving devotion to grief counseling for bereaved parents and advocating for EMDR. To Lola and Walter Green, my heartfelt gratitude for your wisdom and unwavering friendship. Thank you to Joan Chodorow, dear friend and colleague, for sharing your mother's poem, and for your compassion and belief in this book.

To my teachers and mentors, thank you: Arny Mindell, Process Worker/World Worker, who lovingly taught me to find the light in the dark night of the soul; Mary Whitehouse, dance/movement therapist and mentor, who shared her experience and journal after her son Buff died; and June Singer, Jungian analyst, mentor, and friend, who shared her journey of grief and healing after her daughter Judy's death. My gratitude to the teachers at Spirit Rock Meditation Center in the Bay Area and to my colleagues and teachers Jill Mellick and Ellyn Bader. To the Compassionate Friends community, Kara, and Open to Hope Foundation, thank you for your grief support, for offering hope and the knowledge that no one has to walk this path alone.

A special appreciation to family members and close friends who generously agreed to be interviewed for this book. Thank you to David Zenoff, Victor's father, for sharing how it is thirty-seven years later. A big thank-you to cousins Sara Jospin, who inspired me to write this book and was there from the beginning, and Walter Jospin who, with Sara, so graciously shared his intimate family experience of the unspeakable loss in earlier generations. Your unwavering love, support, and encouragement meant so much to me. You are the best! To Sarah Zenoff, my daughter-in-law, my appreciation for welcoming Victor's memory into your family and separating the loss from the love, and to Victoria Zenoff, thank you for your steadfast love. Thank you to my stepdaughter Kate Fay for your valuable insights and for holding Victor in your heart. To all my stepchildren, thank you for being my family and creating more love in my life. I love you.

To my parents, Minty and Abro Robinson, thank you for loving me unconditionally and showing me your resilience. Even after losing your beloved grandson, you counted your blessings in the midst of sorrow. We miss you.

To my loving brother and sister-in-law, Elliott and Gretchen Robinson, my deepest gratitude for your ever-present love and support. You literally made this book possible. You have stood by me through every step with your generosity and encouragement. You wouldn't let me or my book sink, even in difficult times. I thank you with all my heart and am eternally grateful. I love you.

To my daughter Fay and my son Andrew, I began this book when you were teenagers and now I have the blessing of witnessing you grow into wise, mature adults with your own loving families, doing your work to make the world a better place. I have carried with me your wise words:

> Fay: "Mom, this is your life's work, not just a
>   book you are writing."
> Andrew: "Go for it, Mom, no matter what."

Each of you is my teacher and has given invaluable perspective and unending emotional sustenance, memories, humor, and love. Thank you for being you. I love you.

My deep gratitude to my grandchildren, who light up my life every day and fill my heart with lots of laughter and joy beyond words. You are all blessed miracles.

To Steve, my anchor, guiding light, and love, you believed in the book and my dream when I couldn't see the possibility. You provided space for me to work and gave me courage to continue when the task was overwhelming. Thank you with all my heart for your exceptional patience, steadfast support, and understanding, for reading every word and for excellent suggestions and editing, and most of all for your unwavering love. I know Victor would have adored you. I do!

Finally, my most profound gratitude to the universal spirit for the mystery of this life and the amazing resilience of the human heart.